Gotta Tango

Alberto Paz

Valorie Hart

Human Kinetics

Library of Congress Cataloging-in-Publication Data

Paz, Alberto, 1943-
  Gotta tango / Alberto Paz, Valorie Hart.
    p. cm.
  ISBN-13: 978-0-7360-5630-4 (soft cover)
  ISBN-10: 0-7360-5630-0 (soft cover)
  1. Tango (Dance) 2. Tango (Dance)--Argentina. I. Hart, Valorie, 1949- II. Title.
  GV1796.T3P39 2007
  793.3'3--dc22

                                    2006039395

ISBN 10: 0-7360-5630-0
ISBN 13: 978-0-7360-5630-4

Acquisitions Editor: Judy Patterson Wright, PhD; **Developmental Editor:** Leigh Keylock; **Assistant Editor:** Christine Horger; **Copyeditor:** Jan Feeney; **Proofreader:** Joanna Hatzopoulos Portman; **Permission Manager:** Carly Breeding; **Graphic Designer:** Fred Starbird; **Graphic Artist:** Francine Hamerski; **Cover Designer:** Keith Blomberg; **Photographer (cover):** Neil Bernstein; **Photographer (interior):** Neil Bernstein, unless otherwise noted; **Photo Asset Manager:** Laura Fitch; **Art Manager:** Kelly Hendren; **Illustrators:** Alberto Paz, figure 6.3 by Al Wilborn; **Printer:** United Graphics

Human Kinetics books are available at special discounts for bulk purchase. Special editions or book excerpts can also be created to specification. For details, contact the Special Sales Manager at Human Kinetics.

Printed in the United States of America   10 9 8 7 6 5 4 3 2 1

Human Kinetics
Web site: www.HumanKinetics.com

United States: Human Kinetics
P.O. Box 5076
Champaign, IL 61825-5076
800-747-4457
e-mail: humank@hkusa.com

Canada: Human Kinetics
475 Devonshire Road Unit 100
Windsor, ON N8Y 2L5
800-465-7301 (in Canada only)
e-mail: orders@hkcanada.com

Europe: Human Kinetics
107 Bradford Road
Stanningley
Leeds LS28 6AT, United Kingdom
+44 (0) 113 255 5665
e-mail: hk@hkeurope.com

Australia: Human Kinetics
57A Price Avenue
Lower Mitcham, South Australia 5062
08 8277 1555
e-mail: info@hkaustralia.com

New Zealand: Human Kinetics
Division of Sports Distributors NZ Ltd.
P.O. Box 300 226 Albany
North Shore City
Auckland
0064 9 448 1207
e-mail: info@humankinetics.co.nz

Gotta Tango

EX · LIBRIS

First and always for my love Alberto, my partner in the dance of tango and this dance called life, and who is my dear partner in writing and understanding. Then to all our students, our families, our fellow dancers, and to the people of the tango in Buenos Aires who have allowed me to embrace them and the tango.

—Valorie Hart

For my beloved partner in life, dancing, and teaching, my best friend and writer extraordinaire, Valorie Hart. To all those who encourage us, inspire us, and challenge us to want to be better dancers and teachers every time.

—Alberto Paz

Contents

■ Get a glimpse of the history of Argentine tango music and dance and the cycles of agony and ecstasy they have gone through.

■ Get immersed in the evolution of the music, and marvel at the fascination of tango and the people who influenced its essence.

■ Before you run out looking for a partner, learn how to be "tango fit" by preparing your body to be partner friendly.

■ Find out why "to hug or not to hug" is not a matter of choice! Learn about points of contact, and practice the embrace techniques and the concept of *la marca*.

■ Learn all about the rituals and role playing of the tango as you stand up straight, embrace your partner, and begin your journey around the dance floor.

DVD Menu

Total running time: 65 minutes

Foreword

*H*omero Luis ("Acho Manzi") Manzione was born March 6, 1933, in Buenos Aires, Argentina. He is an elected member of SADAIC (Society of Authors and Composers in Buenos Aires) in a supervisory capacity on the auditor's commission. He is well known as a composer of both music and lyrics of tango and folk songs. Acho is the author of tangos such as "El Ultimo Organito" (in cooperation with his late father, Homero Nicolas "Manzi" Manzione) and the lyrics for Cuarteto Cedron's CD, Para que Vos y Yo, produced in Paris. He is also a compiler of poems dedicated to the tango and its influence in the broadcasting and film industries in Argentina. Acho has compiled the prose and short stories of his father, presented and displayed at the XXIV International Book Fair in Buenos Aires in 1998. He has worked in television production and participated in the movie Los Guardianes del Angel (2004).

During the establishment of the tango at the onset of the 20th century, things happened that formed the historical circumstances. The population of immigrants and their descendants had grown in such substantial numbers to take away the country from the conservatives, who had been ruling it at will. The immigrants won the first secret-ballot elections in Argentina, establishing the first populist administration. The people of that generation projected themselves toward the future with the wisdom of their neighborhoods as their most valuable tool. They read from the best texts and studied from the best professors from Europe. Meanwhile, on the street corners, the music and lyrics that had become tango were accompanied by studied steps that sent immigrants and new citizens alike looking for partners at the *milongas*, the fabled gathering halls of early tango dancers.

In 1930, a military takeover snatched the homeland away from the majority and overthrew the government that had protected them. Martial law and a state of siege were the tools used for persecution and repression. That is when Creole wisdom and cleverness resulted in the founding of the social clubs, havens where people could meet during that stifling political reality.

To better disguise their activities, the Creole society hired musicians who, at the same time that the social clubs grew, contributed to the growth of musicians, composers, lyricists, and dancers. There, the milonga was protected while the participants spoke freely of politics and businesses.

Then Carlos Gardel arrived and forged into one all the nationalities. And when much later it seemed that everything succumbed to governmental order, tango was the popular thing that came to save the people. My father, the immortal poet Homero Manzi,* showed me a view of the world of the tango at the apex of its golden age. At no other time did musicians, composers, poets in the form of the lyricist, and dancers converge in one wonderful rush of originality and influence. That is the way my father described the events, as we look at them turning toward the present, with many couples joining their efforts toward education.

Many have reinvented the Argentine tango, and it has even reinvented itself. Just when it had been written off as passé, pronounced dead in newspaper headlines, and ignored by a couple of generations, it came back full force and full circle. There has been a revival, a reinvention of sorts, of the tango in all forms. The golden age is surpassed in sheer numbers of dancers, because the tango has had a global explosion. Credit for this is often given to the most glamorous catalysts in the form of tango shows and tango movies. But a more grassroots influence exists in the form of a handful of protagonists who preserve and foster the tango for the love and respect of it.

Two such persons come in the names of Alberto Paz, an Argentine, and Valorie Hart, a *tanguera* from the United States. Having made the Argentine tango the leitmotiv of their lives, both personally and professionally, these two have promoted the tango to the thousands of students they have touched in the scores of cities and countries in which they have taught their classes. Add to that the thousands of words they have written on the history, the poetry, the music, and the dance in their magazine *El Firulete* and on their Planet Tango Web site, and you come to realize the profound influence these two have proffered to the benefit of the Argentine tango.

Through their exploration, Alberto and Valorie have made the dance form something teachable by expanding on old ideas and codes that permeated the world of the tango when they and others found it languishing for lack of interest and understanding. They have influenced the very language used in teaching the dance. Taking the ideas offered to them personally by proponents of the golden age, they have worked tirelessly to present a clear and accessible construction of the dance. They do this to empower one and all to embrace the enjoyment and benefit of it and to understand the culture and history that formed its music, poetry, and, of course, the dance.

---

*Homero Manzi (1907-1951) was a critically acclaimed poet, filmmaker, author, and lyricist of such classic tangos as "Malena," "Sur," and "Barrio de Tango." In his 44 years he also reached into journalism, teaching, labor, and political militancy with mixed success. The tango lyric was, nevertheless, his true claim to fame and is what keeps his memory alive.

Gotta Tango offers a concise, complete, and clear compendium of the dance of tango, a gift to you, the social dancer, and a must for anyone inclined to become a teacher of it. Nothing like it exists, and it is destined to become a classic, much like the tango itself. This is the fruit of Alberto and Valorie's labor of love and a delightful result of their intelligence and expertise as master teachers.

Acho Manzi
Buenos Aires 2006

Acknowledgments

We extend acknowledgments to tango dancers from just about every state of the union. From 1996 to the present, dancers attended our workshops and hosted us in their homes as we became the first professional tango instructors to travel full time around the United States and eventually join others already teaching in Europe and Asia. We presented a new concept in tango improvisation known as the structure of the tango, which is based on the profound concept of the woman dancing around the man and the man dancing around the floor.

Students provided us with the best research laboratory in which to try out ideas and experiment with a methodology based on common sense and logic. A series called "Tango, Our Dance," which we began publishing in our magazine *El Firulete*, became the laboratory notes, the travel log tutorial, and the basis from which *Gotta Tango* finally was conceived.

We thank Adrian Hutber, one of our students in Champaign, Illinois, for the introduction to Judy Wright, acquisitions editor at Human Kinetics. She took on the project of *Gotta Tango* with such enthusiasm that we finally were convinced that people might actually learn the Argentine tango from a book and a companion DVD.

The idea of acknowledging a city and an act of nature in the context of writing a book is unusual, but New Orleans pre- and post-Hurricane Katrina deserves a special mention. On the last weekend of August 2005, we drove from our home in New Orleans to Tallahassee for a two-day series of workshops. We had just finished the manuscript and were waiting for the copyeditor's review of it. We were focusing on the upcoming shooting of the companion DVD in New Orleans in September 2005. Early on Monday, August 29, 2005, Katrina hit New Orleans, the levees broke, and most of the city was flooded. What Katrina did to New Orleans and our four months in exile played a fundamental role in the way this book went through an epiphany of sorts, the fruits of which you now have in your hands.

The home of David and Hilda Gilchrist in Tallahassee become our home away from home for a whole month. The Tango Society of Tallahassee supported our monthlong tango program. Curtis Rosiek's living room became our private studio for lessons. Thanks to everyone in Tallahassee, we had everything we could hope for under the circumstances: a home, friends, and our job.

Our job travels with us. Tango people from all over the world voiced their concern for our well-being and offered homes and more work. Judy Batista of the Latin Jubilee radio show on the Hudson Valley's WTBQ AM 1110 allowed our voices to be heard after the storm—in New York on the airwaves and by the world on the Internet. Alfonso and Anie Martinez, Sabina Lewis, Jessica Hack, and Edwin Beckman were among the first to return to New Orleans. They reassured us that our home and the precious memories of our life in tango had been spared the brunt of the storm.

In Macon, Georgia, Joyce, and Walt Newman hosted a long weekend of tango for us. Dr. Newman parted with his laptop so we could proceed with our review of the copyedited manuscript and stay in contact with our New Orleans tango community dispersed all over the map.

In Raleigh, North Carolina, Amalia, Roberto, and Tito Restucha received us with a surprise tango party and offered shelter on our way to New York. In the Hudson Valley, Walter and MariLynne Kane hosted a great tango weekend for us as they have done twice a year since 1999.

Julie Stillman, Fardad Michael Serry, and Paul Brombel were generous hosts in Santa Barbara during our miniresidency there. Florentino Guizar and Isabelle Kay invited us to San Diego; Jack and Mary James invited us to Albuquerque; and the Maher Family, the Kucera Family, Cheryl Credio, and Michelle Weese invited us to Arizona.

In Buenos Aires, Daniel Lapadula, Acho and Marilu Manzi, Graciela Gonzalez, Carlos de Chey, and Charlie Daniel were generous and inspirational friends and hosts during the two months we spent dancing, teaching, and visiting the National Archives of Argentina, the late Oscar B. Himschoot's Club de Tango Collection, and mega music store Zivals in search of support material for the book. A special mention to the people at the Conventillo de Lujo, Susana, Cachi, Amy, and Ray, for their heartfelt friendship and generous hospitality.

Our deepest gratitude and respect go to Hugo Lamas and Enrique Binda for their formidable and well-researched book *El Tango en la Sociedad Porteña*, which put within our reach a verifiable and contemporary documentation that narrates a period of the history of tango from 1880 to 1920 where bibliography does not exist.

After returning to New Orleans exactly four months after Katrina, we were relieved to find our archives safe and intact. Our incredible journey, the master classes we gave along the way, and a personal spirit of rebirth made us want to do a complete revision of the manuscript we had already submitted.

We returned several times to Tallahassee, and we decided to shoot the DVD there. Wanda Zubr and Gordon Erlebacher were valuable in their assistance and support for that project.

Finally, thanks to Leigh Keylock, developmental editor at Human Kinetics, for her patience, support, and encouragement during our hiatus.

It's incredible how strong winds and high water can change people's lives. Even though a terrible thing happened, we were able to bring good out of it. What a difference the year after Katrina has made in our lives. We like to think that it happened to us for a reason—that after our four-month tour, teaching with a passion and an inspiration we had not experienced before, we wrote a better book that we hope will become a classic. We're sure *Gotta Tango* is very unique and valuable among the other offerings on bookstore shelves.

Credits

Photos by Jorge Saitta, courtesy of Planet Tango. Pages vi, vii (right), xxi, 167

Photo by Maryann Bates. Page vii (center)

Photos courtesy of Planet Tango. Pages 3, 5, 7, 10, 11, 14, 20-22, 24, 26-31, 63, 73, 74

Photo by Carlos Furman. Courtesy of the Tango Dance Championship. Page 174

Photo by Donna Ferrari, courtesy of Planet Tango. Page 185

Photo by Robert Hubbard, courtesy of Planet Tango. Page 172

© STR/AFP/Getty Images. Page 158

Introduction

To scoop water from the top, the way someone writes what's heard
from others who know from hearing, does not seem safe to me,
neither to formulate ideas, nor to explain with veracity.

—Polibio of Megalopolis (210–128 B.C.)

A car winds its way through the dark streets of a sleepy residential neighborhood, tucked in for the night at the respectable hour of 10 o'clock. Like in postcards, the skyscrapers and bright lights of the city are visible at a distance, taunting the bedroom community of clock-watchers. On nearby hills, the fog rolls in. Here it's clear and the stars are competing with the lights of the skyline for center stage.

After circling around several times, he teases the car into a tight parking spot on a steep incline. She can hardly get out of the car because the pitch of the hill causes the car door to close on her. He runs around to her side of the car and helps her out. Arm in arm, they trudge up the hill. A half-block away, they hear faint sounds of an unusual instrument they know is a *bandoneón*. They quicken their pace. The music has them. Invisible tendrils of wispy arms encircle them and push them upward into the embrace of this delicious sound. They look up into the open windows and see the dancers in the dim light, a *media luz*. They reach the top of the hill now, and the entire city shines in front of them. They are on top of their world. One last look, and in they go, up the dark and winding stairway. Quick hellos, kisses, and hugs; they hurry to change shoes. Their eyes meet and lock onto each other's. He walks to her. She blends into his arms. They breathe deeply, and whoosh, they are on the dance floor, where they will remain for hours and hours, transported, transformed, renewed. They have lived another day to dance the tango.

As romantic as this may sound, like a chapter of charming fiction, this is really the way many Argentine tango dancers feel. There is something so human about the Argentine tango that grabs a primal instinct for human connection, to hold and to be held. All over the world, people are dancing this dance of the people of Buenos Aires with a passion that has been compared to a healthy addiction.

As we do with new dancers when they start their first lessons, we warn you, with a wink and tongue in cheek, that you are about to be exposed to an addictive activity, though a healthy one. Stop now or forever be enthralled in what some call the obsession. Of course you will not resist the temptation to see what this tango obsession and addiction are all about, and thus your journey begins.

The Argentine tango is enjoying a renaissance around the world. Both older and newer generations of social dancers are being inspired by the alluring creativity and natural elegance of a dance form previously perceived as exotic and associated with rose-in-the-teeth and fruit-bowl-on-the-head Hollywood caricatures. Argentine tango is not just another social dance. It cannot be learned in six easy lessons. It cannot be faked on the dance floor. You either know how to dance it or you don't. Its historical and cultural context makes an intriguing and rich counterpoint in the learning process. Its music and poetry, in the form of lyrics, are unique and powerful. No other music sounds like this, and no other dance looks like the Argentine tango.

You should be aware that books and DVDs are not the way most of us learned how to dance the tango. We have discouraged many from solely using those media. While pondering whether to stick to our convictions or to break new ground and pour our experience on paper and digital video, we followed the advice of many who indicated that every tango dancer, man or woman, at any level, owes it to himself or herself to study tango with us at least once—the earlier in one's tango life, the better. There were no exceptions, no qualifiers to that unsolicited statement made public many times by satisfied learners.

So you couldn't have picked a better book than this one written by authors whom many consider to be two of the brightest and most innovative minds among master teachers of Argentine tango in the world. Of course we all tend to exaggerate when trying to impress somebody or make a point. The good news is that if you can read, you can think. If you can think, you can learn the profoundly simple structure on which the Argentine tango is based. Then you can be on your way to impressing anybody, exaggerating as much as your skills develop. Ideally you should read this book with a partner of your choice. However, that is difficult because book reading tends to be an individual activity and tango dancing is a shared partnership. But don't let conventional wisdom stop you. After all, Argentine tango dancers are creative and generous.

Purchasing a second copy to be read in tandem with a partner of your choice would be our first recommendation. Making this copy available to a partner of your choice would probably require a commitment from both partners to take the learning task seriously and to dedicate the necessary time to practice and perfect the newly acquired skills on a dance floor. If you are the partner who's the recipient of a copy of this book, consider yourself lucky because somebody cares enough about you to consider you good tango partner material. Yes, you will need a dance floor on which to practice. It doesn't need to be larger than your living room after you push the furniture against the wall and remove the carpet.

THE FASCINATION OF THE TANGO

The Argentine tango has risen and declined in popularity in Argentina, and around the world, since its beginnings three quarters of the way through the 19th century. At the turn of another century it has become popular again. It has been given a huge boost at the global level through the use of the Internet. It is more popular now than ever: More dancers are dancing outside of Argentina than in Argentina. The music permeates commercials on television and movie soundtracks. Movies about the Argentine tango are becoming a subgenre. Huge Broadway-style tango revues are presented on stages all over the world. What was once seen and experienced only in Argentina is now a part of the entire world.

You probably have some idea of how the Argentine tango might look and how the music might sound. From this point on, you will expand on that initial idea and experience the enjoyable process of becoming an Argentine tango dancer. There are two types of dancers: those who dance professionally for the stage and the majority of dancers who dance socially. The dancer we propose to you is the social dancer.

The Argentine tango strikes an emotional chord in most of the people who practice it. It seems to present itself to many of us at some crossroad of life. When one asks an Argentine tango dancer how he or she came to the tango, it is not unusual to hear themes involving some pivotal point: the passing of a spouse; a divorce; a business failing; the death of a parent; an illness; a recovery of any type; a need to make a life change. It sounds a bit down, but actually it rings true with the genesis of the dance, involving dwellers of a society far removed from their European cradle interacting with disenfranchised inhabitants from the countryside and lonely immigrants looking for the comfort of the embrace. The attraction of the tango is human connection. First we connect to ourselves while connecting with one other person within a socially correct and prescribed embrace. In its sublime ease, the ritual of the tango dance calls for a man and a woman to embrace each other and move together as one around the floor to the rhythm and melody of tango music. While he is moving around the floor, the man is literally carrying his partner in his arms. This is so different from leading and the most difficult concept to understand about

the role of the man in the tango. For the man, it requires confidence and knowledge to navigate the perilous dance floor. For the woman, it requires her to enjoy the luxury of getting the ride of her life.

Another way that people are attracted to the tango is by way of its glamour. They see one of those fantastic stage shows. The orchestra is magnificent, and the music is powerful. The dancers are sexy and sleek and fast on their feet. It is exhilarating. It makes you want to jump up out of your seat. It makes you feel like yelling out, "Hey, I want to do *that*!" This, too, is a powerful emotional reaction.

Tango dancing can be a lifelong experience, an enjoyable way to age gracefully. It is definitely not a means of instant gratification. The important aspects of a systematic process of learning and the hard work that goes along with it should not be discounted. It is also important to keep in mind that the Argentine tango is an urban social dance that has been in existence since the last quarter of the 19th century. Through several generations of dancers, the concepts and elements of the dance have changed as mores have allowed more freedom of interaction between men and women at the social level. How the dance is learned has also changed radically. The way we share information has dramatically shortened the administration of knowledge and the immediate feedback in terms of assimilation of that knowledge.

Just a few years ago, the thought of learning to dance the tango from a book would have been ludicrous and branded as a very useless idea. We began to change our allegiance to that school of thought after we found ourselves keeping in touch with our students around the world via the Internet and a magazine. We had to figure out ways to convey and reinforce concepts using the written word and people's power of imagination. You are now the beneficiary of that experience, and we expect you to make us proud by becoming a good dancer. During the learning process, both men and women need to understand that we will be role-playing, and the responsibilities of each role on the dance floor are quite different.

First, we must assume control over our own bodies to acquire good balance, which translates to finding the correct axis in order to develop the most comfortable posture. Second, both the man and the woman must learn and understand the concept of using body language to communicate. This is a concept unique to the tango and is known in the native language of the tango as *la marca*. This concept is essential for getting the exhilarating experience of improvising on the dance floor.

IN EVERY TANGO, A STORY

The Argentine tango can be enjoyed individually. One of the greatest achievements is for a man to be able to dance with any woman who knows how to dance, and for a woman to be able to dance with any man who knows how to dance, anywhere, anytime. The tango brings people together for a variety of reasons: life crises, soul searching, and the glamour and exhilaration of being able to dance for the love of it. We are among those life partners who were captivated by the tango. One of us is from Argentina; one of us is from the United States.

We both learned the dance as adults. Because of the intense early experiences we shared, we made a life-altering decision to change our professional and personal paths for a tango lifestyle. We now devote our full time to fostering and promoting the dance, the culture, the music, and the history of the Argentine tango. At the time of this writing we have accumulated 25 years of combined experience. Our partnership began in 1995.

When we started our learning process, we were in the same predicament as you might be now: curious, a little scared, and very hungry for good instruction in the dance. When we started there were no books, or magazines, or movies, or even Argentine tango music on CD, and certainly no Web sites. The only teachers at the time were connected with a show, *Tango Argentino*, touring everywhere. They might be in one city for a day or two or maybe even a week. The audiences were so enthralled that some who were determined went backstage and implored any couple from the cast who could understand English or high school Spanish to teach them how to dance that way! A few hurried lessons whetted the appetite and left the novice desperate for more lessons, but alas the show had left town.

As the revolving doors of our city brought a variety of dancers teaching the flavor-of-the-month patterns, our appetite for logical knowledge made us wonder if somewhere in the old neighborhoods of Buenos Aires somebody knew how the structure of the dance came about. After all, our professional minds were certain that such an intricate way to dance had to have some foundation, some structure that was based on common sense. We were seeing (and taking classes with) many natural social dancers and a few show dancers who were starting to teach. Some had no idea how they did the beautiful things they did, and they certainly had no way to communicate this to their students. "Let me show you how I do it," they'd say. Then they'd repeat, "Just do what I do." After minutes that felt like hours, they'd review, "Let me show you again how I do it."

We learned by watching the dancer or teacher show a step time after time. When we couldn't grasp the concept, he or she would show the step again. And then they would show it again and again. If we were lucky enough to be able to imitate what we were looking at, the lesson was deemed a success. Every Argentine tango dancer has a unique way of expressing the same movements. So to the untrained eye, it seemed that there were thousands of different steps presented by hundreds of different teachers. We might learn a step in a certain way, and then another teacher would say, "No, no, no," and tell us to do it his way, with his style. It was a mess. Then we became aware of the existence of master teachers in Buenos Aires who had danced at the end of the golden age (1930s to 1950s). This was a generation of dancers who learned from those who developed the structure of the dance we currently do. As we began our search for knowledge we realized that all that existed was an oral body of knowledge based on those foundations. The experience of those who knew, referred to as *el yeite*, was bound by a code of honor that dancers from the first part of the 20th century abided by: "We don't teach anybody what we do." It seems that generation after generation of dancers have learned by observing others and then finding ways to do the same thing in a different way! We soon learned that in the Argentine tango, imitation is the worst kind of flattery!

Our learning experience in Buenos Aires began with an acknowledgment of the existence of a structure based on a logical grouping of a finite number of movements that could be executed in an infinite number of ways. Sometime in the late 1930s a new generation of dancers set out to try new ideas and movements to catch up with the evolution of the music. They created new patterns that added proactive participation of the female dancer. These men changed the way the tango had been danced until that point, and that is pretty much the foundation of the way we are dancing Argentine tango today.

When we first entered an austere room on the upper floor of an abandoned naval museum, we were driven by the desire to learn the latest figures and become the greatest tango dancers the United States had ever seen. Almost immediately we experienced a reality check, and sooner than later we realized that we were not going to learn how to dance but rather learn how to think. We then spent hours staring at invisible trajectories and lines drawn with a finger on a bare wall. Grueling drills followed the lectures as our bodies struggled to accommodate the instructions from the brain. We didn't know what to think or what we were in for. Several long weeks later, after hours of daily classes, we realized that we had acquired an incredible wealth of knowledge and a clear understanding of the structure of the dance. We had the know-how to improvise on the dance floor and to teach it in the classroom. It took us another year to get our bodies to respond to what our minds wanted. We have continued with years of enjoyable exploration. We always find some other nuance as we up the ante with the sublime simplicity that produces such beautiful complexities between two dancers. This knowledge made it possible for us to learn and to teach others how to take a class and benefit from any material presented by any dancer or teacher and execute it with ease and total understanding. Soon people began to notice our ability to dance with ease and style, and they began to ask us to show them what we knew. Because we also had a solid pedagogy, our reputation as clear and fair teachers was quickly established.

As we evolved as teachers and matured as dancers, we took the unique oral education that we learned in Buenos Aires and refined it and expanded on it. We developed a structured methodology enhanced by our life experiences in the world of the engineer, the artist and ballet dancer, and the soccer player and coach. We started writing about it in a magazine about the Argentine tango that we published, *El Firulete*, in a series of articles titled "Tango, Our Dance." This series had grown to nearly 30 chapters by the time we were commissioned to write this book. Those chapters were shared with everyone on our Web site (www.planet-tango.com/ourdance.htm), and it got us noticed worldwide. Many younger teaching stars acquired their bases and vocabulary from the pages of "Tango, Our Dance." From these articles, we began to receive invitations to teach all over the United States and the world. We have taught in the Philippines and in Buenos Aires. We have been teaching in Europe in Lisbon, London, Hamburg, Utrecht, and in the mountains in Umbria. And we always teach wherever we live and hang up our dance shoes at the end of the night. At the time of this writing, our shoes are hanging in Buenos Aires and New Orleans, a sister city in feeling to Buenos Aires.

THE PROCESS OF LEARNING

The most obvious and important thing we have observed as we have traveled the world to teach is that the human body is built the same for all of us, and it works in the same way. We also see that the learning process is the same for everyone—young or old, man or woman.

At the beginning, most people approach learning tango by looking at the feet of the teachers as they show "the steps," aiming their video cameras at the floor. This way of learning how to dance is characteristic of just about any dance except tango, where looking at the floor and focusing on the feet are quick giveaways of a beginner status. We urge you to raise your eyes off the floor and learn by looking with your eyes and ears. *Listen* to the instruction, *look* at the way the bodies interact in three dimensions, and *do* (not sit or just watch) what you are being asked to do. An exceptional book like this and its companion DVD cannot substitute for the live classroom experience with a qualified teacher. They are an excellent primer and a teaser that will make you want to seek more and more personal experiences. We hope you continue to experience the pleasure and privilege of this addiction called the Argentine tango.

Besides being a how-to book, this is an encapsulation of the culture and history that formed the Argentine tango. Again, when we started, there were very few books on the subject written in Spanish and certainly nothing in English. Now, there are many more books in both languages and even several videos presenting dance instruction. Unfortunately, most published aspects related to the formative period of the tango (1880 to 1920) have not been based on verifiable documentation. As a result of that, a copious bibliography talks about improbable events that are repeated and embellished intentionally, thanks to the lack of rigorous and methodical investigation on the subject.

This is not meant to be a history book. However, since many books written about the "history" of tango are based on folklore, tall tales, and biased prejudices, we want to contribute our conclusions. They are based on a chronological wealth of research and investigation verifiable and available in Buenos Aires at the *Archivo General de la Nación* (National General Archives), *Archivos de la Policía Federal* (Federal Police Archives), and the *Biblioteca Nacional* (National Library). We hope to make a connection for you to Argentina and the Buenos Aires society of the 19th century that framed the genesis of the genre of the dance you want to learn. We don't expect you to want to become *porteños* (inhabitants of the port city, what the people of Buenos Aires are called and call themselves). But we hope that you will develop a respect, and even affection, for the country and culture that now present you with the gift of this experience that will enrich your life forever. Embracing the story of the tango and keeping it alive within you will add meaning and richness to your dancing experience.

Learning this dance is not easy, though the movements are natural and not difficult when you let them happen. However, it requires that you work, that you take possession of your body and comport it with responsibility. It requires that you work in a partnership, each contributing 100 percent. Because the process has no shortcuts, there is an abundance of gimmicks being peddled as the secret way to learn. Save yourself time, energy, and grief, and accept that if you want to learn to dance any dance, there is work involved. With the Argentine tango, the work might seem a little harder, because this is dancing at its fundamental level. If you open your mind to think, try not to be neurotic, and use your reasoning and life skills, you will progress fast enough to take to the social floor in a short time. We don't promise that you will be the best dancer that you can be right away, but you will be able to dance in a social situation in a convincing way. Remember, this dance is a longevity form. This is something you can enjoy your whole lifetime, and it will help you be the better dancer and person for it.

Our opinions are strongly formed and stated. We assume you are an adult, and we'll treat you that way. If you have come to disagree with us, you will do so. If you come with openness and listen to what we say, you will learn how to dance using the fundamentals of the Argentine tango. Fundamentals are not something you learn today and then discard tomorrow. Accomplished musicians do scales. Accomplished athletes do drills. Accomplished ballet dancers do daily classes at the *barre*. Accomplished artists draw every day. Accomplished writers write every day. This is how you use your fundamentals. They are the tools that you will use every day as a tango dancer. The more experienced you become, the more your fundamentals will look so spectacular that they will not be recognized as such by the untrained eye.

There is nothing easy about fundamentals. Still we must all start at the beginning. Every time you step up to take each other in your arms and go to the dance floor, you are beginning again. In this sense we are all beginners forever. Cherish this present time on your learning curve. You will feel the exhilaration of the new and the glow of accomplishment. The fantastic thing about the Argentine tango is that these feelings can be felt, again and again, with every tango you dance, with each passing year.

We expect you, at this point, to be intrigued enough to read on about dancing tango, to learn it, to dance it, and to enjoy it. Tango is the ultimate touch dance between a man and a woman. It is a safe form for experiencing human connection three minutes at a time. It is an exercise in mutual respect and consideration for both partners as they both embark on a journey that requires full participation and cooperation from both ends of the partnership.

The challenge for you, dear *tanguero* in the rough, is to raise your eyes from the floor where legs and feet intertwine in complex and unpredictable patterns, and to look at the sublime language of the bodies as they blend into natural turns navigating the expanse of the dance floor to the beat of the music, in perfect harmony with the melody. This is how you'll learn from us as we speak together to present to you our individual viewpoints on what makes up the unique partnership that forms the tango. Tango is all about improvisation. To improvise, you must have the tools, the blueprints, and the appropriate instructions that teach you how to use them to make your tango dancing excel.

Before you run out seeking a partner, prepare yourself to be tango fit and trim. Become acquainted with every element of your body so that you learn how to use it to become a pleasant, graceful, and partner-friendly dancer.

Each lesson is visually illustrated in the accompanying DVD. First you will see the individual exercise, and then you will see how it works with a partner in a real dance situation. Remember that this is all about dancing. Dancing requires practice, and practice makes perfect.

Turn the page, and let us now start. . . .

PART

I

The Intrigue of the Tango

The Everlasting Tango

Words like tango are empty holders that everyone fills in accordance to their feelings and their knowledge, generally using the latter for the benefit of the former.

—*José Gobello,* Tangueces y lunfardismos de la cumbia villera
(Corregidor 2003)

The tango made an unexpected reappearance in Buenos Aires, Argentina, in the 1980s, when the South American country was reeling from one of the darkest periods of political, economic, and social unrest in its history. It was a horrifying time span that began in 1976. The significance of the renewed interest in tango is that it confirmed the resiliency and everlasting attributes of a phenomenon that, across many generations, has surged to incredible peaks of popularity followed by crushing chasms in which all indications pointed to its irremediable death.

For many, the mention of the word *tango* first brings to mind the image of the dance, or of dancers doing the tango. While the mere word *tango* has evoked vivid images universally for many years, for the previous two or three generations it has remained a dance form relegated to theatrical shows and movies. A majority of contemporary dancers have had their inspiration sparked by the sizzling images of slit skirts, stiletto heels, and intricate legwork performed at lightning speed on stages around the world. In the early 1980s, the only presence of tango in Buenos Aires was primarily a product designed for export, dispensed in nightclub shows for consumption by tourists.

Guillermina Quiroga and Alberto Catala performing at the New Orleans Tangofest.

It was only after the successful run of the musical revue *Tango Argentino* worldwide that tango and Buenos Aires became a magnet for tango tourists interested in learning how to dance. Other musicals followed suit: *Tango Pasión*, *Tango × 2*, *Una Noche de Tango*, *Perfumes de Tango*, and *Forever Tango*. In the mid-1990s British filmmaker Sally Potter delivered *The Tango Lesson*, a mostly black-and-white film that chronicled the experiences of a mature British woman trying to learn to dance the tango. Then Carlos Saura released his own film, *Tango*, about a filmmaker making a film about tango. Robert Duvall, a confessed tango addict, wrote, directed, and produced *Assassination Tango*, a thriller about a hired killer (played by Duvall himself) who becomes fascinated by the tango in Buenos Aires. International, national, and regional shows, films, DVDs, CDs, and even books with a tango theme are all part of the life-support components of tango lovers, tango fans, tango addicts—in other words, *tangueros*, so-named to describe those who make the tango an integral part of their lives in its various manifestations.

GENESIS AND MYSTERY

There is a popular quote attributed to the late orchestra director Anibal Troilo: "The tango is discovered little by little, and it chooses us. When it does, it gives us a glimpse, but it remains, as it has forever, surrounded by a halo of impregnable mystery." So how important is it to know where it was played and danced initially? Who were the musicians and the dancers? How did the dance look and the music sound? What were the cultural and moral values of the society where the gestation of the genre took place? We believe that knowledge of these facts is important because it helps to demystify the great number of urban legends about the origins of the tango that were used as excuses for all kinds of exploitation. From knowledge comes the understanding and tolerance of the cultural traits and rituals that explain the way the tango is learned and danced. Keeping an open mind and exercising respect for those cultural traditions are the first steps to becoming a considerate tango dancer.

It would be worthless to discuss the definition of the air we breathe in order to be able to breathe. Defining it by attributes such as its temperature, purity, or density would be mistaking essence with attributes. Air is the fluid that forms the atmosphere of our planet. The embrace, connection, and musicality are often described as essential ingredients of the tango in order to justify using tango choreography to dance to music other than tango music. Those attributes are common to many other forms of dancing but do not define the essence of the tango.

To define the tango in essence is an irresolvable difficulty, because no one has been able to witness its genesis and live long enough to leave any accurate testimony on record. Tall tales about its marginal character, its lubricious choreography associated with men dancing with men or with prostitutes, or sad thoughts that can be danced could be accepted as attributes but by no means as a definition. One thing is certain, by the end of the 19th century a pheno-menon called tango existed in Buenos Aires. To this day nobody knows exactly what it was like. As a dance it appears to have had a choreography whose steps were shared with other dancing rhythms. Evidently people then had a notion of what was meant by tango as a musical genre, but they didn't leave any messages buried in time capsules to be opened at a future date. One thing that is certain is that since the end of the 19th century, the people of Argentina have been dancing tango to music purposely composed for dancing the tango.

It All Began With Spain

Dancing is one time-honored way of establishing relationships between the sexes. Colonial Buenos Aires inherited from Spain an addiction to dancing as well as the rulers' concern with regulating the interaction between the sexes. A concern for legislating the consequences of activities involving sexual themes such as dancing goes back to the origins of the city of Buenos Aires. The *porteño* (the attribute of things or people from the port city of Buenos Aires) society had guidelines and laws. The government made use of legislative, preventive, repressive, and enforcement apparatuses to establish its will over the people. The events that led to the origins of the tango happened within that society and therefore within a framework of coexistence. It was not isolated in houses of ill repute frequented by men and women of questionable morals and virtues.

The revolution that set in motion the process of independence of Argentina began on May 25, 1810. There is evidence from newspaper and magazine accounts shortly afterward that people danced socially in private and public salons, in theaters and tents, during carnival time, and during outdoor religious holidays (called *romerías*) that lasted for weeks.

Revelers of the *porteño* society during *romería* time.

> **porteño—An inhabitant of the port city of Buenos Aires.**

People also danced in places designated as *academias de baile* (dance academies) that appeared as early as 1826 and offered to teach all sorts of dances. Soon, it became obvious that the so-called dance schools didn't teach anything; they were places where all sorts of people gathered to drink and dance. Residential homes, academias, and legal brothels were located next to one another in the central areas of the city. Public inebriation and rowdy behavior upset and annoyed the families who lived in the neighborhood. The sale of liquor at the dance academies and the resulting inebriation of patrons brought about regulations, fines, and taxes on public dances. These dances became the main targets of prosecution by the police. Tough enforcement of the regulations resulted in the proliferation of clandestine academies. Starting in 1859, there is evidence that dancing took place in some brothels; however there is no indication that people there danced anything different than what others were dancing elsewhere. In other words, there was dancing at some brothels before there was any hint of the existence of anything called tango.

The Natives Just Want to Have Fun

Throughout the 19th century, journalists pandered to the elite class of cattle ranchers and landowners. They appointed themselves as moral monitors of good manners, denouncing the "indecent and immoral ways" of dancing popular rhythms with abrupt interruptions of the flow of the dance while the dancers executed steps in place (*cortes*) and exaggerated swaying of the upper body (*quebradas*). These styles of dancing were favored by the populace and eagerly imitated by the rest of society. Yet, the *corte* and *quebrada* were not essentially Argentine inventions or exclusive attributes of the tango. Those rare dance figures who seemed to scandalize the moralistic chroniclers of the 1880s had been observed in Andalusia, Milan, Tuscany, Paris, Marseille, and London. The European dancing modalities adopted in Buenos Aires were danced by all elements of society.

The inhabitants of Buenos Aires had been dancing the *vals* (Spanish for *waltz*) since the early days of the 19th century. The polka arrived in Buenos Aires via Paris in 1845. The schottische and the mazurka also became known before 1852. Halfway through the 1860s Spanish zarzuela companies introduced the habanera, and it soon became a popular dance. The habanera suffered a curious mutation in its designation. It began to be known as tango *americano* to differentiate it from the tango *español*, although it's not clear why the perfectly identified name was changed for another that required a qualifying adjective to avoid confusion.

The most peculiar musicians in the early 19th century were the street harpists who carried a portable version of the instrument. They could be found in trios that included a flutist and a violinist, cruising the streets and stopping at hotels,

An organillero and his organito.

delighting their audiences with precious pieces of music from the best operas, and charging by the song. They were mostly Italian musicians, and by the 1870s they advertised their services for "dancing and having fun." Tango mythology books associate the origin of tango music with illiterate itinerant musicians who played their instruments by ear.

In the early 1880s there was still no evidence of anything called tango being danced by the public. The popularity of the so-called *organito*, actually a street organ grinder, cannot be ignored. The organito, which dates back to as early as 1837, was not a conventional instrument. It was like a player piano that mechanically reproduced programmed music. It did not need a musician, just somebody who transported it and made it work by turning a handle. Organ grinders were the most popular source of music for dancing, with a repertoire that included the rhythms of vals, polka, mazurka, schottische, habanera, milonga, and folk music from the interior of Argentina. There were also instances in which some sort of can-can and the cakewalk were danced.

Programming the music for the organitos required the ability to read sheet music, and writing sheet music required an academic knowledge of music theory. While some of the primitive tangos were propagated by the organitos, one of the biggest urban legends credits illiterate musicians with creating the early tango by playing their instruments by ear.

Drinking and Dancing Don't Mix

To get an idea of what a clandestine dance academy was like, open your mind to images that may not be present in the world you know. Visualize a time and place in 19th-century Buenos Aires. Here is a reading from a police report that recommends shutting down one of those establishments because of a violation of the edict that made it illegal to dance at a place where liquor was served:

> . . . Each time the door opened, the noise of feet shuffling on the floor could be heard from the other room, as if many people walked dragging their feet. Behind that door there was a great salon where people

danced some quite original dances. On the far wall of the salon there was one of those organ pianos, covered with a mattress. The mattress had the purpose of preventing the sounds from reaching the street, or even the room in front. The muffled hits of the instrument's hammers evenly marked the tempo of the song that was being danced with a strange noise resembling an instrument of percussion on wet wood.

With that strange music they dance in the salon. And they dance with two, three, or four women who are hired by the owner as dancers. These unfortunate women dance all night long. Every night, without resting, they go from the arms of a Creole dancer who twists them in a milonga, to the arms of a Briton who shakes them dryly in a jumped vals, to the arms of an Italian who dislocates their bones with a syncopated rhythm.

The salon is packed with dancers and since the women are few, the rest dance man with man to take advantage of and not waste the song that somebody else has paid for. At the end of the song, somebody shouts, "*Lata!*" That means that he claims his turn to pick the next song. He approaches the *organillero* (organ player) to request his favorite piece, he pays for the song, and he gets a tin token (*lata*) for the piece that he requested. And the dance continues in a warm atmosphere because the room is closed, the smoke of the cigarettes clouds the air, and the brushing of the feet on the floor is the dominant noise. Everybody is quiet; nobody talks because they are there to dance. There are no chairs in the salon so as to discourage loitering; those who enter must dance or leave. (From Hugo Lamas and Enrique Binda, 1998, *El tango en la sociedad porteña, 1880-1920* [Buenos Aires, Argentina: Hector Lorenzo Lucci Ediciones], 35-36.)

We hope you notice the absence of bloody fights among dagger-wielding thugs and whores pulling switchblades from their garter belts. It's becoming evident that those who have dedicated their time to writing about the tango and its origin have not been interested in the popular medium, but only in its marginal aspect, the forbidden part. This makes their body of work historically irrelevant, as it is not representative of the entire porteño society.

By the end of the 19th century, overcrowding in the large tenements, caused by massive immigration, made the sidewalks an extension of the social activities of the dwellers. Dancing on street corners came into vogue. Entrepreneurial young men hired a couple of organ players and taught passing young girls to dance in exchange for the girls paying the organ player for each piece of music. In many neighborhoods, it wasn't unusual that the lack of gender balance led to "bread-with-bread" practicing (that is, people of the same sex going through the learning process on the sidewalks and hallways in anticipation of the real dances at salons, recreation centers, private clubs, theaters, cafes, and restaurants).

TRADITION AND EVOLUTION

Popular bands of professional musicians were sought after to animate banquets, celebrations, dedication ceremonies, and carnival dances. Some of these bands were among the first musical ensembles to record early tangos between 1907 and 1914. The invention of sound recording and preparations for the centennial celebration of Argentina's liberation from Spanish rule at the turn of the century signaled a period of popular acceptance for a more defined and recognized genre identified as tango. A large number of schooled musicians from the zarzuela companies composed a similarly large number of tangos, many of which were recorded by bands of 20 and 30 professors. In 1912 the recordings of bands suddenly seemed to disappear. At the same time there were many recordings by typical orchestras that featured a new instrument of German origin from the concertina family, the *bandoneón*. Records, as primitive as they may have been initially, required expensive machines to play them. Those who could afford the luxury owned record players and bought records. We can assume that the more affluent part of society accepted and encouraged the composition and recording of tangos, which they bought as quickly as music stores offered them. This fact contradicts tall tales about the marginalization of the tango by society and its development in sordid environments by economically disenfranchised people with no musical knowledge.

> **bandoneón**—*A concertina looking reed musical instrument originally created as a portable pipe organ for music for outdoor religious activities in Germany. It has the appearance of a box with bellows with two sets of buttons, one for each hand.*

The Music Business Begins

The first 30 years of the 20th century sum up the creative process of the tango both in technical and musical terms. Primitive mechanical systems acoustically recorded early music. The first electrical recordings started in 1926. These were undoubtedly the best decades of tango, a time of amazing production both in terms of quantity and quality of songs played by numerous performers. For the first time, tango became successful outside its birthplace, reaching audiences in Europe and the rest of Latin America and North America. Great composers such as Rosendo Mendizabal, Angel Villoldo, Ernesto Saborido, Eduardo Arolas, Ernesto Ponzio, Agustin Bardi, Gerardo Matos Rodriguez, and Vicente Greco created some of their best work during this period. They composed timeless classics such as "El entrerriano," "La cumparsita," "El choclo," "La morocha," "Don Juan," "El lloron," "Que noche," "La cachila," and "Ojos negros."

The world's most prominent recording companies set up shop in Buenos Aires, and Argentina's own recording companies started to grow at a very fast pace. Tango was the world's favorite social dance. The tango as an exotic novelty took Europe by storm. Musicians traveled to Paris, and many stayed there. Skilled dancers found job opportunities in the City of Lights as dance instructors for rich Parisian socialites.

The furor over the tango in the dance halls and nightclubs of Paris was at first condemned by an elitist Argentine ambassador who swore that no decent Argentine would ever practice a dance spawned by the element that patronized the brothels of Buenos Aires. There has never been an attempt to find out how the ambassador knew what was going on at the houses of ill repute in his beloved Buenos Aires. Nevertheless, halfway through the first decade of the new century, the ruling class in Buenos Aires began to warm again to the tango because of their desire to be part of European society. They set out to replicate the ambiance of the European nightspots where they could dance the tango while removed from the lower-class immigrants who had made the tango part of their social milieu. The first European-style cabarets in Buenos Aires began to appear around 1916, and the tango became the ruler of the nights of Buenos Aires.

Tango Is Also Music

During this period, the music of tango began its first major evolution, led by a new generation of conservatory-trained musicians of mostly immigrant descent. These musicians banded together under the claim that tango was also music. The middle of the 1920s saw the evolution of a tango that was primarily music, characterized by a rich and melodic content with a 4/8 time signature. It was a popular music that was always composed beforehand and played with a prior agreement by standard tango orchestras. Music, dance, verses, and instrumental interpretation became established as the four arts making up the tango.

The "look" that Parisian dancers gave to the tango.

For 30 years after the festivities celebrating the first hundred years of Argentina as a nation, the film and recording industries, along with stage plays and radio broadcasting, saturated every corner of Buenos Aires with the sound of the tango. The coverage expanded to the interior of Argentina as well as to Latin American and European nations. People listened to the music with an almost religious reverence. Orchestras and singers were awarded idol status by their loyal followers. The dance was embraced with a passion, and the verses of the most popular tangos were on the lips of every proud inhabitant of Buenos Aires.

THE ESSENCE OF A SONG THAT ENDURES

The Great Depression of 1929, the advent of sound in films, and the tragic death of Argentina's most famous tango singer, Carlos Gardel, in 1935 signaled a period in which the tango was even declared dead in a newspaper headline. It was a period of mourning that prepared a new generation for one of the greatest periods in the history of the tango.

Carlos Gardel.

Carlos Gardel, born Charles Romuald Gardes in Toulouse, France, popularized the lyrics of tango songs in Europe and Latin America. He is an icon in Argentina, where popular lore says that he sings better every day. He was part of a trilogy (with Maurice Chevalier and Bing Crosby) of great protagonists of musical films. Gardel is credited with having sung the first tango on stage in 1917, catapulting the popularity of tango lyrics to unexpected heights and literally creating a new genre, the tango *canción* (tango song). After touring Spain and France, he became popular around the world as a tango singer. His tragic death on the tarmac of the Medellin, Colombia, airport shocked the nation of Argentina. Several months later, when his charred remains were returned to Buenos Aires, funeral services lasted for days. His coffin was transported 40 city blocks to his final resting place at the Chacarita cemetery, accompanied by thousands of mourners on foot. Thousands more threw flowers from balconies along Corrientes Street. People from all over the world still visit his tomb, where his likeness is portrayed in a life-sized bronze statue preserving his eternal smile.

In 1937, a maverick bandleader named Juan D'Arienzo helped launch a significant period for the tango. He defied the musical canons established in the mid-1920s and revived the old standards from the beginning of the century. Using a rigid tempo, his music sent droves of dancers into frenzy as they crowded into cabarets and dance clubs. For his technically simple interpretation of classic tangos with a celebrated instrumental precision, D'Arienzo was dubbed the King of the Beat.

The resulting cultural and economic impact favored the onset of the golden years of tango. Radio stations competed fiercely to attract audiences by featuring the best tango orchestras. Large social clubs contributed to the tango euphoria by opening their huge dance floors to tango dancers. Thousands of couples demanded more and better music for dancing, and scores of orchestras obliged at cabarets, nightclubs, cafes, sports clubs, and recording studios and on the airwaves all over the country.

In the 1940s World War II distracted the U.S. entertainment industry from promoting their music abroad. In that vacuum, as Argentina remained neutral, the 1940s unleashed a period of glory for the tango and its music. These golden years were the pivotal time in history when the tango dance, the music, and the poetry reached every corner of the city of Buenos Aires, traveled across the interior of Argentina, and crossed the borders into most of Latin America. There was very little influence from the rest of the world, which was preoccupied with the war. As a result, the art form was kept in a rare state of purity and authenticity. The dramatic changes in the music, the dance, and the poetry of the tango once again matched the structural and social changes of the city of Buenos Aires.

The urban demographic of the 1900s, with five men to each woman, had long disappeared. However, the way in which couples resolved conflicts in life as well as in tango was still ingrained in their psyches. What had changed was that women were no longer the exclusive targets of blame for disappointments in love. Men shared the blame as well as the responsibilities and consequences of failure. The new generation of poets of the tango displayed in their lyrics an entirely new body of work that acutely reflected the transformations in ethics, anguishes, and hopes prevalent not just in Argentina but also worldwide.

In remarkable contrast to the generation of immigrants that descended from the planks of ocean-crossing vessels in the 1870s, the young generation that ruled the tango in the 1940s came from nearby provinces such as Buenos Aires, Córdoba, and Santa Fé. They immigrated to the capital city of Buenos Aires, bringing along a meticulous musical education. They looked out for one another, rooming together in boarding houses that soon became filled with the sounds of their instruments. The inspiration of these musicians as a whole was uninhibited. The fruits of their unusual talent resulted in an orgy of melodies that enhanced the repertoire of the best orchestras, delighting audiences with spectacular tangos, valses, and milongas. They introduced the tango singer as a human instrument. Meanwhile, a new generation of dancers began to incorporate new concepts in order to differentiate themselves, since copying steps from other dancers was against the strict codes of conduct prevailing at the dance halls. Men and women developed a discreet and intimate way to invite, accept, or reject an invitation to dance. It was eye contact and *cabeceo*, or nod, a subtle movement of the head (*cabeza*) from a distance. Men sought the best female dancers and vice versa, because part of tango dancing involved honor, prestige, and a desire to look the best on the dance floor. This required that both men and women first learn to dance

> **cabeceo**—*A nodding movement signifying "Shall we dance?" prevalent at the traditional dance halls of Buenos Aires. The gesture is used by the man as an invitation to a lady, who allows eye contact to be made from a distance. A lady's nodding of the head, or any other subtle facial movement, indicates "Yes, you may dance with me."*

well before attending a dance hall. The first public dances most men and women attended were with friends and relatives in a rite of passage into the world of the dance halls of Buenos Aires.

The ritual for asking, accepting, or refusing to dance afforded a distinct advantage to the female dancers. Prospective partners were judged on the basis of their skills, demeanor, and grooming. The ladies were seated in prominent areas around the dance floor based on a protocol that took into consideration their experience and reputation. From their vantage point, the women could assess the pool of male dancers. An invitation was allowed by making eye contact with the candidate. The men standing by the bar, or seated in special bullpens according to their reputation and seniority, scanned the room to make eye contact with those ladies who either had a reputation as dancers or had shown their skills on the dance floor.

As a man scanned the room, a connection might be made with a gazing lady. The man would nod his head in a silent invitation. Upon receiving the assurance of a gentle nod, a subtle smile, or a deliberate batting of the eyelashes, he would begin the journey toward her table with his eyes locked onto hers. This was necessary to avoid embarrassing situations in which more than one suitor might have misinterpreted and intercepted a lady's green light.

When the man reached the table, then and only then would the lady stand up and take one step onto the dance floor, waiting for the man to stop in front of her. He would raise his left arm, offering his open hand, palm up, to gently wrap her hand with his fingers. She would then raise her left arm to allow him to embrace her while she rested her left arm on his shoulder. Then they would take a side step to the left of the man and begin to move into the line of dance. This action of getting onto the dance floor was expressed in Spanish as *salir a bailar*, which translates as exiting to the dance floor, to begin the dance.

A NEW WAVE OF FOREIGN MUSIC

Throughout the 1940s and '50s, the popular music of Buenos Aires coexisted in the great dance halls with foreign rhythms such as the foxtrot, bolero, rumba, and jazz. Above all, the rhythm of the tango and its lyrics were always present on the airwaves, at the theater, in the movie houses, in the printed media, at the downtown tea houses, at the cabarets, at both grand and modest neighborhood clubs, and of course at the exclusive hangouts called *milongas* where patrons listened to and danced only tangos, valses, and milongas.

Throughout the late 1950s and the 1960s the recording companies were back in force and the tango began to languish. It was replaced by a succession of dances coming from pop music and rock 'n' roll. Until then, the recording companies had been making money reproducing the sounds that people sang in their homes and wanted to hear on records they bought. That applied equally to classical and popular music. Once the recording labels exhausted everything that could be remembered, improvements in technical quality kept making money for the companies without adding anything in terms of novelty. Soon more improvements such as long-playing records (LPs) came to satisfy listeners, but the recording industry eventually ran out of material and it set out to invent a form of music that could be repackaged in a variety of ways with a massive marketing campaign aimed at the younger generations. The priority of the industry being focused on ways to rake in profits seems to be the reason that recording executives ordered the destruction of master recordings of all the tangos that had been recorded at the studios of RCA Victor of Buenos Aires.

> **milonga**—*May refer to the music, written in 6/8 time, or to the dance itself, or to the dance salon where people go to dance tango, or to a tango dance party.*

Contrasting settings at a cabaret and a milonga at a social club in the 1940s.

Around 1956, the recording industry created the new wave, *la nueva ola*. It was a massive marketing campaign that resulted in the sly conversion of the long-standing tango and jazz clubs into extra-large concert venues. Nobody could dance there because space was at a premium. Acho Manzi, a veteran popular poet, commented with sarcasm on the subject: "They even did away with our carnival celebrations, in addition to silencing the whistling from the streets."

A Show Named *Tango Argentino*

The current revival of the tango has spread with blazing intensity, thanks to the globalization of communications. It started to rise around 1990, after 30 years of no major tango activity, with the unexpected success of a musical revue aptly named *Tango Argentino*. Producers Carlos Segovia and Héctor Orezzoli synthesized all the implicit dramatic qualities of the tango on the stage. They focused on the taciturn man of Buenos Aires (who is secretly idealistic with a devastating sense of humor) and the seductive Buenos Aires woman (who is alluring and drop-dead elegant). But it was the performance of the dancing couples that captivated the public's imagination, reintroducing a dance in which the man flaunted his masculinity and the couples embraced each other in a sensual ritual full of irresistible beauty.

What is most fortunate is that we are dancing the original dance—the Argentine tango—worldwide. The offshoot dances of American and international tango are still being danced at large. There has never been a time in history when so many social dancers are dancing Argentine tango as it was danced in the golden years of the 1940s and '50s. As globalization has affected every aspect of life; it has also happened with the Argentine tango.

Where's the Beat?

Let's fast-forward to today. Most people can recognize a tango when they hear it—especially the ones that have become standards and have been used in countless movies and shows. But after listening to those two or three well-known tangos and being exposed to the huge body of music that is the Argentine tango, new non-Argentine dancers still often struggle to hear "the beat."

The instrumentation of the players is unique. The biggest distinction is that there are no drums. (Note that when some orchestras play for Broadway-style shows, they may introduce a drum set for a more amplified sound, but in general there are no percussion instruments.) The classic line-up would include piano, violin, bass, and a unique instrument called the bandoneón.

There is an entire separate set of tales regarding the appearance of the bandoneón in Buenos Aires. Since sailors and immigrants arrived by the thousands late in the 19th century, it is conceivable that some of them may have brought bandoneóns to Argentina. It is believed that this German instrument was originally designed as a portable organ for outdoor religious activities. It fits together nicely with the other popular components brought to the tango by the immigrant culture. Eventually the bandoneón replaced the flute and clarinet, rapidly managing to capture the entire range of emotions that musicians, poets, and dancers express in their interpretation of the tango.

Tango was, is, and will continue to be the music of Buenos Aires, while permanently sharing itself with the world. It reflects the life experiences of the people who served as a model for its birth, growth, and maturity. Through various periods, the dance and the music collided, as proponents of a musical evolution alienated the dancers bent on preserving the traditions. Long periods of popularity closely associated with the dance preceded and followed periods of fracture when experimentation, new ideas, and generational changes of guard set the stage for yet another cycle. All along, the dance itself has maintained an evolving structure that is closely associated with the music. The ability to understand, appreciate, and respect the music of tango is a very important quality that goes a long way in developing a good tango dancer.

CHAPTER 2

Tango and Nothing Else

Bandoneón, what do you name her so much for? Don't you see that the heart wants to forget, but she returns, night after night, as a song in the teardrops of your weeping sound . . .

—Homero Manzi, "Tango che bandoneón" (1949)

They say that on certain nights when the moon is full, and the fog rolls in like a cotton shroud from the banks of the River Plate in Buenos Aires, a late-night walker might suddenly hear the moaning sound of a bandoneón. Looking up, the walker would recognize the face of Anibal Troilo on the surface of the moon. Anibal Troilo was one of the most revered bandoneón players of the golden years. He was, and still is in memory, the most distinguished bandoneón player of Buenos Aires. The bandoneón is the instrument that best expresses the complex set of emotions embedded in the tango and symbolizes the image of the music itself around the world.

For tango dancers, a deep knowledge of the music is essential for strolling on unlimited journeys through dreams and memories. Many great musicians have left the distinctive sounds of their instruments for posterity, along with the unique touches of their inspiration. Their musical legacy comprises the complex set of rhythms and melodies that keep tango dancers addicted and excited from beginning to end on any given night of tango dancing.

Cultural values definitely affect the way people express and deal with emotions. Many cultures consider the expression of emotions a sign of weakness. In the tango culture, the weak are those who are not capable of facing and expressing their own emotions, because they will be ill equipped to deal with the feelings of others.

As you step into the world of the tango, your emotions and your perception of the emotions will take a unique twist according to who you are. Only you are capable of expressing the intense emotions that the music, the dance, and the sight of others dancing may stir in your heart. Tango devoid of emotion can quickly become an empty exercise in geometry.

If you have not been raised listening to tango music day in and day out, you may recognize a tango when you hear the European versions of "Hernando's Hideaway," "Jealousy," or similar tunes played with accordions, strings, and drums to accentuate the beat. Hollywood and the media in general have perpetuated the stereotype of the tango as an exotic manifestation that evokes dips and lunges, or as a caricature of brilliantine-coiffed Latin lovers mistreating fishnet-clad, slit-skirted, stiletto-wearing prostitutes on stage. If you are curious enough to try the Argentine tango, you'll soon find that tango musicians call their groups orchestras, not bands. The rhythm section lacks percussion instruments. The subtle but unmistakable beat is kept by the left hand of the piano, the plucking of the strings of the upright bass, maybe a guitar, and definitely the bandoneón.

The compositions created through the genius of Astor Piazzolla in the late 1950s have caused much confusion regarding the nature of tango music. Although he started with the traditional structure of the tango, Piazzolla soon deviated from the modernizing currents inspired by the likes of Horacio Salgan and Osvaldo Pugliese. He began by removing all vestiges of the characteristic tango beat, the rhythm that attracted dancers as an audience. He proposed a more symphonic sound that was designed to keep the less educated tango dancers away. Piazzolla himself facetiously dubbed the new sound "music of Buenos Aires." It was pitched initially to the intellectual elite, at popular cafe concert establishments, and eventually to an international audience who made Piazzolla a star.

Unfortunately, Piazzolla alienated the popes of the tango establishment in Buenos Aires, who never forgave him for treating them and the genre with disrespect. He finessed the worldwide recognition of the tango as a representation of the popular culture of Buenos Aires while furthering an agenda of experimentation with sounds that nobody would have recognized as tango if controversy and slick publicity copy had not defined it as *tango nuevo* (new tango) or *tango de vanguardia* (vanguard tango). He capitalized on the controversy, appealing to those who found established traditions and popular cultural assertions too difficult to understand, accept, and respect.

There is something unique in the way we learn about tango music. When one learns to identify most forms of music, one of the first questions asked is, "What's the name of that song?" In the tango, while the name of the tango is indeed important, the more important question is, "What's the name of the orchestra?" This is not as unusual as it seems. There was a similar occurrence in the swing and big band era. People could identify the sounds of the orchestras led by Glenn Miller, Benny Goodman, Artie Shaw, or the dozens of others that existed then.

At first it might seem overwhelming to have to think about the hundreds of tango orchestras that stamped their personal style on the tango firmament. Relax and find reassurance that, as with any form, the top 5 or 10 names come easily to the forefront. This is where we will start tuning our ears. Since we are dancers, we will listen to the best of tango music composed and played for dancing. A steady beat, *el compás* of the tango is what the dancers want.

compás—*The main pulse that defines the tempo of the music.*

THE LEGENDARY TYPICAL SEXTET

One of the apparent reasons for the lack of historical data regarding the evolution of tango music at the turn of the 20th century is the way the government dealt with the massive immigration that swelled the tight quarters of Buenos Aires beginning in the 1870s. Public opinion, still haunted by the memories of the devastating epidemic of 1871, when yellow fever wiped out almost 10 percent of the population, demanded strict regulations against any foreign presence suspected of being carriers of the feared germs. A new ruling class in 1880 set out to get rid of what they saw as a menace to the moral health of the new nation. They were officials involved in the game of inclusion and exclusion, deciding who would be part of the building of the country and who would not.

The scientific branch framed into academic thesis a conspiracy to make exclusion simply a matter of science, not race. The preoccupation of the science, the arts, the police, the state, and the army was with what they saw on the streets of Buenos Aires, where the underworld made its presence felt through prostitution, anarchism, sexual inversion, and tango. A number of edicts made it a violation, punishable by fines and imprisonment, to cross dress and to dance with members of the same sex in public or in private. During those dark years, the tango danced in the underworld became the backdrop to a treacherous violation of civil rights against those suspected of a gay lifestyle. This has fed the frenzy to pass as fact urban legends about a period of proscription, of a "forbidden tango," of a tango that "first was a men's dance," and a tango that was "born in the brothel."

As another generation came of age, a new political truce resulted in the adult male population acquiring the right to use the secret ballot. A popular government was elected for the first time. The tango, having conquered Paris and all of Europe, found its tarnished image cleansed. The porteño elite financed and built Paris-style cabarets around the city for dancing tango while distanced from the lower class. Their wealth handsomely underwrote a number of first-class orchestras, among which Osvaldo Fresedo's became a symbol of that period. Musicians fully enjoyed an unsurpassed period of prosperity for the musical genre that identified itself with the pulse of a growing and changing population.

The establishment of the *sexteto típico* (the typical sextet consisting of two bandoneóns, two violins, a piano, and a counterbass) took place in the mid-1920s. Most chronicles indicate that there was a condescending attitude toward the traditional orchestras that continued to play strictly for the dancers. Many published historians, in pontificating and elitist discourses, associated the dance of tango with a lackluster, monotonous way to play the tango by groups lacking the artistic motivation to explore further than the dancer's feet. The decade that followed was a period of greatness for the development of tango music intended for listening as well as for dancing.

For the "academics" of tango (who never ventured into the world of the dance as practitioners), the evolutionary period that started in the mid-1920s when Julio De Caro took over the six-piece orchestra led by Juan Carlos Cobián was a period of splendor and renaissance for tango music. A new generation of well-trained musicians distinguished themselves among the countless sextets that appeared everywhere. Many went on to form their own great orchestras in the golden years. Experts say that the most genuine form of expressing the tango in an instrumental manner resided within the sexteto típico.

The depth and breadth of the tango as an art form are sometimes overlooked from a historical point of view, because up until now, no serious accounts of its history have been undertaken from the dancer's point of view. But it is precisely the dancer who is in a position to explore the rich body of music that spans generations of composers and musicians. As dancers take to the dance floor, they write new chapters of history with every step, and give more equitable credit to everyone who ever created great music over a distinctive rhythm. In New Orleans, everybody knows that a gumbo without a roux is just another soup, and we firmly believe that Argentine tango without its native rhythm is just another piece of music. There is no doubt that dancing continued during the 1920s, a decade that led to the first major crisis of the tango. The wealthy and those aspiring to the good life found the cabaret a natural habitat in which to enjoy nightlife. Buenos Aires became a replica of Paris and Montmartre: Cabarets named Armenonville, Royal Pigall, Maxim's, Tabarin, and Montmartre illuminated the porteño night.

The original Julio De Caro Sexteto Típico: (left to right) Julio De Caro, Francisco De Caro, Pedro Maffia, Enrique Krausse, Pedro Laurenz, and Emilio De Caro.

The "good life" at the cabaret in Buenos Aires in the 1920s.

CARLOS DI SARLI, THE LORD OF THE TANGO

As previously explained, the tango beat is marked by the left hand on the piano and the finger picking of the bass. One of the great piano men of the tango is Carlos Di Sarli. Serene, restrained, self-confident, and demanding, Carlos Di Sarli knew, as nobody else did, how to conduct his orchestra from the piano. He combined rhythmic cadences with a deceptively simple harmonic structure to create a unique style of tango music full of nuances that continues to inspire dancers the world over. He was born in Bahia Blanca, a port city on the southern tip of the province of Buenos Aires, which he immortalized in a popular tango of the same name.

Di Sarli wore dark glasses for most of his life to hide the damage caused by the accidental discharge of a firearm at his father's gun shop. His dark glasses and reserved demeanor fueled unfair and unfounded innuendos. Saying his name was considered bad luck (*yeta*). This caused him considerable grief throughout his controversial artistic life.

Di Sarli's legacy stands today, as it did during the golden years of the tango. He is the only orchestra director who did not belong to either of the two prevailing schools of his time: the traditionalist school of Roberto Firpo and Francisco Canaro or the evolutionist school led by Julio De Caro. His was the essential definition of uniqueness—a school of its own, which never graduated any followers. Carlos Di Sarli's sound was, and still remains, unique.

Carlos Di Sarli, the lord of the tango.

Born on January 7, 1903, Di Sarli was the eighth of nine brothers born of immigrant parents (Italian father, Uruguayan mother) who worked very hard to keep a roof over their heads and food on the table. Among his elder brothers were a music professor, a baritone, and a piano player. His brothers had a great influence in his decision to enroll at a conservatory at an early age. By the time he was 13, he had mastered the piano and the works of the classics. However, tango music was everywhere, and he soon felt inclined toward the popular genre.

Di Sarli put together his first orchestra when he was 16 years old. He played mostly in and around Bahia Blanca until he turned 20, when he moved to Buenos Aires. Details of Carlos Di Sarli's personal life from this point until the time of his death in 1960 are sketchy, filled with hearsay and misinformation, and generally absent from the existing literature of tango. It is clear that his personality was overwhelming, and it flowed musically through the classic pealing of his right fingers on the keyboard. He adorned the tango with a meticulous orchestration while faithfully preserving the original spirit of the creators. Traditionalist and romantic, he was and still remains the proponent of a very personal style, for which he will always be recognized as *El Señor del Tango*, the undisputed lord of the tango.

For many critics of the time, Di Sarli's traditional and deceivingly simple concepts did not have much value, except for dancers. The legacy of Carlos Di Sarli is at least twofold. He instilled in his orchestras a sacred flame that made them different from every other orchestra. That flame elevated the dancing of tango to its summit. He conducted his orchestra from the piano with a scheme generally characterized by the lack of instrumental solos. You can listen to the bandoneóns sing the melody at times, but they also mark a rhythmic and danceable beat. Occasionally a violin ventures in, in an extremely delicate way, for a brief solo or a countermelody. The piano always leads, with an embellished bass line that clearly emphasizes the first of the four beats. This is a trademark of the maestro, linking the bars of the piece and stressing the delicate, elegant rhythm, primarily for dancing.

El Señor del Tango was absolutely respectful of the melody and the spirit of the composers of his repertoire. He embellished the orchestral instrumentation with subtle details, avoiding the false contradiction that existed between the evocative traditional tango and the avant-garde. Carlos Di Sarli was the final piece of the puzzle of tango in the 1940s, which made concessions neither to strident fashions nor to rhythmic extravagances. He represented, with extreme delicacy, the interpretive paradigm of tango for the ultimate pleasure of dancing.

Selected Recordings of Carlos Di Sarli

Bahia Blanca	Bar Exposición	Los 33 Orientales
Comme Il Faut	Milonguero Viejo	Di Di
A la Gran Muñeca	Mi Refugio	Re Fa Si
El Ingeniero	La Cachila	Quejas de Bandoneón
Don Juan	El Cachafáz	La Cumparsita
El Amanecer	El Choclo	La Mulateada
El Once	Cara Sucia	Zorzal
El Caburé	Nueve Puntos	Yo Soy de San Telmo
El Distinguido Ciudadano	Champagne Tango	

JUAN D'ARIENZO, THE KING OF THE BEAT

The decade of the 1930s in Argentina was marked by strong political instability, which resulted in the military overthrow of the first constitutionally elected president. The Great Depression also had damaging consequences for the economy. And to top it off, singer Carlos Gardel was killed in a plane accident on June 24, 1935, while on tour to promote his latest movie.

Carlos Gardel, who had been singing for more than 20 years, had created another layer of tango followers, those who listened to the tango. Composers and poets produced an enormous amount of work, which Gardel made popular through recordings, in musical revues on stage, and in the movies after he became an international star who toured Europe, South America, and the United States. His unexpected death in 1935 contributed to a national sense of gloom that was exploited by foreign record and movie companies, eager to cash in on the entertainment value offered by films and international rhythms. These events affected the nation in a very negative way, and the consequences were also felt in the tango world.

There was already a major war going on between the followers of two schools of thought of tango. The traditionalists and the evolutionists had been waging a quasi-religious war since the second decade of the 20th century. It had to do with the music, or the way the tango was played and why. The only remaining bastion of the tango was the growing number of radio stations that competed for the services of the most popular directors to lead the orchestras that identified each radio station. Still, most orchestras had become stale, uninspiring, and tediously slow. A turning point came about in 1934, when a mediocre violin player named Juan D'Arienzo gave up playing the instrument forever, his agile and expressive arm becoming his conductor's baton. D'Arienzo went against the prevailing slow style, creating a different interpretation, and basing his repertoire on compositions from the old guard that had been discarded by the trendsetters of the 1920s. He replaced pianist

Carnival dance with live orchestra sitting in the mouth of the mask.

Luis Visca with an up-and-coming journeyman named Rodolfo Biagi in 1937. The originality and ability of Biagi to accelerate the rhythm of the orchestra with the dexterity of his fingers created a combination that became an overnight success over the airwaves.

The resurrection of the tango happened at one of the most difficult moments in its history. A new crop of dancers who previously felt disaffected was attracted back to the dance floors at the following year's carnival celebrations. These crowds followed the D'Arienzo orchestra everywhere, anxious to dance again to the contagious Creole beat. The success of D'Arienzo's simple interpretative concept completely revitalized orchestras during the second half of the 1930s. From that moment on, success never deserted him. Countless orchestras followed suit, trying to imitate the nervous and emphatic beat popularized by D'Arienzo. This process laid the foundation for the great tango boom of the 1940s, a revival that paralleled what had happened during the first two decades of the century.

Juan D'Arienzo felt the tango in its old-fashioned way and was totally aware that he was not inventing anything that had not already been invented. He did not think that he had the right to alter the original form of tango. So he went back to the source of the traditional

Juan D'Arienzo, the king of the beat.

tango, looking for its old prestige and its own enchantments. In spite of all the obstacles that were opposing its return, he brought it back to the place that he thought the tango honestly and rightfully belonged. Although he carried his success all the way to the bank and forced a revitalization that led to the golden years, the academics never gave D'Arienzo a place in their writings, except to compare his music to the banging of pots and pans.

In spite of the many detractors, the tango had its king. As the king of the beat, D'Arienzo proved to be a crucial innovator and a man of artistic genius. The recognition he received throughout his career is the people's eternal testimony to one of tango's most illustrious interpreters. If it's correct to say that the style of D'Arienzo did not contribute any significant aesthetic element, it's also true that the popular response to his artistry signaled an approval that no other orchestra had ever achieved. It has been up to tango dancers all over the world to reaffirm the recognition that dancers gave D'Arienzo in his time, naming him *El Rey del Compás*, the undisputed king of the beat. This is an orchestra that dancers should include in their collection of tango music.

Selected Recordings of Juan D'Arienzo

El Rey Del Compás	Tucumán	Gran Hotel Victoria
Sábado Inglés	El Pollito	9 de Julio
Maipo	El Marne	Loca
Comme Il Faut	El Internado	Por Qué Razón
Ataniche	Don Juan	C.T.V.
El Flete	Que Noche	El Buey Solo
Yapeyú	El Chamuyo	La Chiflada
Rawson	El Arroyito	Este Es el Rey
Joaquina	El Opio	La Cumparsita
Independencia	La Puñalada	Milonga, Vieja Milonga

OSVALDO PUGLIESE, THE MASTER

On December 2, 2005, there were major celebrations in honor of what would have been the 100th birthday of Osvaldo Pugliese. A small square of the city was dedicated to Osvaldo Pugliese and named after him. A life-sized sculpture of his orchestra was unveiled, and a free concert featuring alumni of the various Pugliese orchestras took place in a fenced-off alley next to the square.

Pugliese passed away on July 25, 1995, after a lifetime of achievements and disappointments. Pugliese is credited with taking the tango to the pinnacle of instrumental interpretation. But his life was also marked by persecution and imprisonment because of his political convictions. Having waited too long while he was alive, a group of people known as the Friends of Osvaldo Pugliese started the celebrations on the night of August 14, 2001.

People walking on Corrientes Avenue near the doors of the Teatro Alvear had to dodge their way around lines of men and women that extended around the block and into Lavalle Street. It was a typical evening in the midst of a typical Buenos Aires winter. During August, as has been the curse of the country since the colonial days of the 18th century, what occupied people's minds were the high cost of living, the drop in

Life-sized sculpture of Osvaldo Pugliese dedicated on December 2, 2005.

the value of salaries, the devaluation of currency, external debt, corruption at the official levels, the rising crime rate, and how to survive another recession. There were no special announcements in sight that would have given the casual stroller a clue as to why people were standing in line, some from the early hours of the afternoon. The next day Mauro Apicella would report in the newspaper *La Nación* that the organizers of the event had lacked optimism to gauge the public response to an offer of a free tango concert launching a cycle of activities called *Pugliese Vivo, 2001-2005*. Three times as many people as the Alvear Theater can accommodate attended, making it difficult for those who already had tickets to gain access to their seats.

The Friends of Osvaldo Pugliese, organized as a permanent homage commission, took the initiative to pay tribute to the grand master. They laid out an ambitious program of activities that included concerts, exposition of plastic arts, literature, and of course music associated with the tango. Only the fanatical followers of the artistic life of Osvaldo Pugliese remember that his debut with his *Orquesta Típica* took place on August 14, 1939, at the Café El Nacional. The date chosen to launch the *Pugliese Vivo, 2001-2005* cycle seemed capricious to the majority, but for those who knew, it marked the 62nd anniversary of that celebrated debut. It is the published objective of the commission to rescue the philosophy of the dearly beloved *maestro* along with his preoccupation for exalting the music of the city.

Perhaps the most authentic proof of a teacher's legacy is the achievements of his disciples. Pugliese was a teacher who influenced a star-studded generation of musicians, most of whom are still alive. He was also an exemplary father, rewarded with the gift of a daughter who followed in his footsteps. Beba Pugliese sits today at the piano, the way her father did, at the helm of a gifted group of musicians. She was, on that night of the commemorative concert, a Pugliese at the piano, leading a monster line-up of bandoneón players and violinists in the grand finale of "La Yumba," the signature tango that defines the sound of a music that reflects the plight of a city and its people from the creative genius of Osvaldo Pugliese.

Osvaldo Pugliese, as the son of Italian immigrants, was inspired to study music by his father, an amateur tango flute player. Initially Osvaldo studied the violin, but he soon switched to the piano, showing an enormous talent at a very young age. At age 15 he joined a tango group, and thus began an illustrious career that would eventually make him the greatest tango musician of the 20th century.

Until 1934, Pugliese made several attempts to form his own orchestra. He joined violinist Alfredo Gobbi and young bandoneón player Aníbal Troilo for short-term engagements that included radio broadcasts. Then, bandoneón player Pedro Laurenz—ex-member of De Caro's sexteto típico—decided to form his own orchestra. He called Pugliese to sit at the piano. In 1936 he played for bandoneón player Miguel Calo. Throughout his ascending career, Osvaldo Pugliese was acutely aware of the political and economic crisis that had divided Argentina's population. In particular, musicians did not have a voice in decisions that affected their jobs and compensation. When Pugliese finally decided to go out on his own, he set up his orchestra as a cooperative, modeled perhaps after leftist ideals that he felt attracted to. Everyone had an equitable participation, not only in the distribution of income but also in the

Pugliese seated at the piano, in the early years.

Pugliese orchestra at the Teatro Colon in 1986.

creation of arrangements and composition of new titles. The results Pugliese achieved contrasted dramatically with the unjust persecution and incarceration that regime after regime perpetrated against his unassuming figure.

The debut of Osvaldo Pugliese's first stable orchestra took place on August 14, 1939, at legendary Café El Nacional. Osvaldo Ruggiero on bandoneón, Enrique Camerano on violin, and Aniceto Rossi on bass contributed to the distinctive sound and style that have characterized all the Pugliese orchestras ever since. Fortunately, his legacy has been preserved in 450 recordings and by generations of musicians that continue to project his genius and humility into the new millennium. The recording cycle started on July 15, 1943 (with "Farol" and "El Rodeo"), and ended on March 26, 1986, with "El Encopao," live at the Teatro Colon.

Pugliese became the most advanced exponent of the school first proposed by Julio De Caro, incorporating a strong beat that proved that tango music could appeal to dancers without sacrificing quality. Long before Horacio Salgán and Astor Piazzolla started to experiment with counterpoint (one or more independent melodies added above or below a given melody) and syncopation (stressing of the weak beat), Pugliese had made these musical features an integral part of his innovative sound. He re-created the masterpieces from both early and contemporary composers (Arolas, Bardi, Cobian, De Caro, Maffia, Laurenz, Canaro, Firpo, Scarpino, and Piazzolla). His musicians also contributed significant compositions of their own. Among Pugliese's recordings, 35 percent were instrumental, and he or members of his orchestra composed 50 percent.

On Thursday, July 27, 1995, the skies of Buenos Aires were menacingly dark, but they did not cry. A multitude of men and women who had been shouting for over four decades, "Don't ever die, Pugliese!" did all the crying. Two days earlier, Osvaldo Pugliese had peacefully entered immortality. The absurd way in which Argentines conveniently forget the atrocities committed against the lives of those who, like Osvaldo Pugliese, refused to sell out their convictions, gave way to open demonstrations of sorrow. Another myth was being born. Red flowers, a symbol of his absence while imprisoned, colored the collective mourning one last time. Five bandoneóns paid their everlasting respect to Osvaldo Pugliese, moaning and weeping the sound of his sound, forever recognized, remembered, and applauded as *"La Yumba."*

Osvaldo Pugliese, the modern master.

The sound of the Osvaldo Pugliese orchestras spans four decades, each one with a distinctive characteristic that seems to match the social and political transformation of Argentina from the 1940s to the 1980s. The first orchestra in the 1940s brought the sounds and arrangements of the sexteto típico to their highest expression. In successive decades, the rich sound of the orchestra acquired the distinctive rhythmic structure that makes dancing to Pugliese a sublime accomplishment for those who reach that level of mastery. This is a state of mind that is totally understandable from an insider's viewpoint.

Selected Recordings of Osvaldo Pugliese

Recuerdo	La Yumba	N.N.
Farol	Negracha	Seguime Si Podes
La Rayuela	Malandraca	Arrabal
La Mariposa	Remembranzas	Chacabuqueando
Emancipación	Gallo Ciego	Mala Junta
A Evaristo Carriego	Nochero Soy	A los Amigos

ANIBAL TROILO, THE PREMIER BANDONEÓN OF BUENOS AIRES

For many, Anibal Troilo is the archetype of the 1940s tango. Somehow, among the many luminaries that emerged during the golden years, Anibal Troilo has been elevated to the category of myth. This explains why his artistic achievements, his musical prowess, and his personal life have been chronicled in many oblique ways, the way religious writings deal with the unexplainable mystery of faith. Ironically, though having been dubbed in the early 1960s *"el bandoneón mayor de Buenos Aires* (the premier bandoneón of Buenos Aires)" by poet Julian Centeya (a moniker widely accepted and adopted as dogma), his name does not seem to generate excitement among dancers outside Buenos Aires. The sound of his orchestras does not seem to be as recognizable as those of Di Sarli, D'Arienzo, or Pugliese. The challenge presented by the *sabor troileano*, the Troilo zest, to inexpert dancers is proof of the need for qualified tango teachers to pave the way to what is an acquired taste.

Young Anibal Troilo.

As should be expected, in Buenos Aires, generations of *bailarines de tango*, the tango dancers, have been embroidering invisible arabesques on the floors of neighborhood clubs and downtown cabarets to the rhythm of Pichuco (Troilo's nickname) for several generations. Anibal Troilo's musical life spans two different periods, separated by a year when he did not perform live or on the radio. The first period began in 1937, when he put together his first orchestra, and lasted until 1954. The second era began in 1956, with the incorporation of vocalists Roberto Goyeneche and Angel Cárdenas, and lasted until his death on May 18, 1975. A careful analysis of both periods reveals several important developments that could be defined as revolutions if we were talking of events that affected society as a whole. Instead, let's talk about innovations, influences, and the audacity to confront the complacency of the establishment.

bailarin—A dedicated dancer.

Troilo began as a graduate of the evolutionary musical school led by Julio De Caro. Midway through the 1920s, Julio De Caro set the standard for the sexteto típico. The Decarean style had defined roles for each instrument, an aristocratic sense of importance, and an audience that belonged to or pretended to belong to the aristocratic segment of the society. The roles of the instruments in the Decarean style of tango interpretation were strictly defined. Some had a responsibility for the melody while others were assigned to keep the rhythm. Anibal Troilo added a counterpoint to his first arrangements, highlighting his own bandoneón solos. In a constant state of evolution, the Troilean orchestra began adding functional variants that altered the traditional Decarean root with totally new nuances. One of them was the transferable duty of the instruments. The piano, for example, was generally used for marking the rhythm, but it also enjoyed solos of melodic phrasing. The bandoneóns, while typically playing the melody and sustaining the harmonic structure, often took on the strict marking of the rhythm. The egalitarian and interchangeable roles of the Anibal Troilo orchestra reflected a cross-section of the public who danced to his music in an environment characterized by its egalitarian consistency, the social club. The road leading to the formation of his first orchestra in 1937 was full of character-forming experiences, for a man who would become a myth and for a musician who would become an icon.

Anibal Carmelo Troilo was born in Buenos Aires on July 11, 1914. Times were hard; the voices of the newspaper boys reminded everyone about the world at war. Adding to the images of pain, sadness, and poverty that shook his fragile early life was the death of his sister shortly after he was born. By the time he was eight years old, his life would become mournful with the death of his father. His mother would assume the bread-winning role for the family by opening a storefront stand selling candy and cigarettes. Many years later, Troilo recounted, "The tango reached me through Gardel. One night while burning with fever in bed, my mother put a Gardel record on the record player and the tango got into me like a fire. Later she bought me a bandoneón."

Troilo began to take bandoneón lessons at age 10. After six months he could play easy tunes. In 1925, at the age of 11, he auditioned and got a job in the house orchestra of a popular movie theater that provided the musical background for silent films. In 1937, Anibal Troilo accepted an offer to play at the dance club Café Marabu. The advertising for his July 1 debut promised that the Troilo orchestra would surely delight the dancers with its rhythm.

Anibal Troilo, the premier bandoneón of Buenos Aires.

The word that describes the Troilo style is *complete*. His solos demonstrate a sound that does not need technical jargon. He was not narcissistic, ostentatious, or exhibitionistic; the bandoneón in his hands, held on his knee, hardly moved. The stage lights would dim, leaving him alone in the spotlight with the mystery of his romance with the instrument. Those who have seen him and heard him can only describe the experience as the deep eruption of emotions that occurs when the magic of his sound takes possession of the body. Among the many merits attributed to Anibal Troilo were his intuition in selecting his musicians and singers and his ability to adapt them to his ensemble. The selection of his repertoire also indicates his brilliance. His favorite composer was himself. Forty-one of his recordings were his own.

Toward the end of his career, Anibal Troilo fell victim to a lifestyle that many have tried to tone down with euphemisms, as if excesses in eating, drinking, and recreational drug use had anything to do with the fact that his music defined the *porteño* sound of the tango. We choose to remember Anibal Troilo as a romantic, sensitive, and humble human being. The alcohol consumed at the tin counters of many bars drowned his soul, battered by the pain of many losses. In the quiet hours of many late-night encounters, the alcohol and the absurdity of untimely deaths of family members and dear friends turned into tears that poured easily from his squinting eyes.

The life of Anibal Troilo moved around heartaches. A mild stroke had affected him seriously a year before his death. For 20 years he dealt with the excruciating pain caused by an arthritic hip. He once went through hundreds of cortisone shots within a 60-day period. On the morning of May 18, 1975, Troilo fainted, and spent most of the day in intensive care at the Hospital Italiano. That evening, around 8 p.m., patrons were filing into the doors of the Teatro Odeon for a performance of the musical *Simplemente . . . Pichuco* (Simply Pichuco). However, that evening the show didn't go on. At 11:40 p.m. the heart of Anibal Troilo played its final note. The torture of the man had come to an end. The peace of his soul had begun. The city mourned the death of an idol baptized on the sidewalks with the teardrops of his sobbing bandoneón.

Selected Recordings of Anibal Troilo

Quejas de Bandoneón	Cachirulo	Responso
Milongueando en el 40	Toda Mi Vida	Sur
Guapeando	La Tablada	Malena
Cordon de Oro	Tinta Verde	Barrio de Tango
	Romance de Barrio	La Mariposa

BECOMING A TANGO CONNOISSEUR

If you spend time listening to and recognizing the distinctive sounds and styles of these four orchestras (Di Sarli, D'Arienzo, Pugliese, and Troilo), you will find it easier to relate to their particular ways of playing and composing tango music. Each had a long career influenced by personal growth and changing times. Within these repertoires are *milongas* and *valses*, sister and brother rhythms of the tango that make up the trilogy of music danced at tango parties. Included in their works is the voice of the tango singer, contributing another aspect of preferences and identification. In all of this richness, you will also come to learn the names of the tangos. As time goes on, you will discover your favorites and want to listen to more music.

There is another aspect of the music: the written lyric. Tango lyrics are considered poetry, with each era preserving a verbal snapshot of its time. Some lyrics are classics, beloved for their timelessness and universality as well as the beauty of their language. Fortunately for the non-Spanish speaker, translations are published in tango magazines and Web sites (such as Planet Tango at www.planet-tango.com/letras.htm).

While some dancers find it distracting to hear vocals or dislike tango with lyrics, the classic dance orchestras introduced the singer during the middle or last portion of the song, using the voice as another instrument of the orchestra. Some tangos and singers are strictly for listening to. The more typical musical arrangements feature the vocalist at the forefront of the song. The epitome of the tango singer for Argentines is Carlos Gardel. His humble origins and further success have made Gardel the archetypical rags-to-riches dream of every disenfranchised man from the working class. Such is the reverence that people profess for Carlos Gardel that the complete absence of Gardel's voice at the dance halls seems very odd to many foreigners.

This is another example of the multidimensional range of the tango. An entire sector of the population listens with reverence to the dulcet tones and beautiful words of the immortal voice of Carlos Gardel. To get up and dance to his voice is unthinkable. For that reason Carlos Gardel vocals are never played at a social dance. One of the foremost requirements of any tango promoter, teacher, or facilitator is to become educated in all the aspects that make up the cultural framework of Argentine tango.

As you will see, we dance to an amazing array of recorded music. Other dances, such as swing or salsa, make use of live music when possible. Living musicians are playing Argentine tango music worldwide, but they are fewer in number than in other popular forms of music. The main reason is that the bandoneón, the instrument that gives the tango its special sound and accent, is a vintage instrument that is difficult to master. Furthermore, it is difficult to use it to express the genuine touch and feel of the men and women of Buenos Aires. It takes a deep understanding of the porteño soul to be able to play tango on the bandoneón with the proper accent.

There are still players remaining from the latter part of the golden years. They primarily play in Argentina and occasionally travel outside the country for special presentations and shows. The cost to mount such productions is staggering. European, Japanese, and North American orchestras do exist, but on a limited basis because the remuneration is small for the amount of effort it takes to learn the instrument, play and maintain it, and keep a group going. Until recently most live music was played for the concert—for listening only. Dancers always drew a low card, because dance music wasn't considered artistic enough for the serious musician. Times have changed, since it is the dancer who has successfully brought the revival of the tango to a worldwide level. More and more musicians want to play for dancers because it is often their only opportunity to play. Dancers have become more discerning, having been raised on the recordings of the best orchestras of the tango. Live music must be good (that is, it must have the beat and be well played) in order for the dancers to support local groups or visiting orchestras.

Start Your Tango CD Collection

Over the years we have listened to thousands of tangos—first on old 78s and vinyl, then on audiocassettes brought from Buenos Aires, and finally from a collection of CDs acquired methodically as they became commercially available.

The first serious efforts to market tango music on CDs appeared toward the end of the 1990s. After that, many labels appeared, and larger record stores began to carry a selection of Argentine tango music. Buyers should beware that authentic music for dancing is hard to come by, except through specialized sites that either stock the classics (D'Arienzo, Troilo, Di Sarli, Pugliese, Calo, Tanturi, Biagi, D'Agostino, Gobbi, Canaro, De Caro) or offer compilations created by tango music experts for the dancing pleasure of their customers.

Tango is music to be danced, just as much as it is a dance done to the music of tango. In the beginning it was the dance that led the music as the early composers wrote and played for dancers. Eventually the music caught up, and in turn, it led the dance. The various styles of the greatest orchestras not only defined generations but also formed the bases for allegiances. Beginning in the late 1920s and extending well into the 1960s, dancers showed preferences for particular orchestras and their characteristic sounds. Since the start of the renaissance in the 1980s, dancers have shown an expanded tolerance for a diversity of orchestras and sounds, making an evening of tango dancing a journey through time and a celebration of the joy of dancing tango.

How to Dance the Argentine Tango

It Takes You to Tango

All we actually have is our body and its muscles that allow us to be under our own power.

—*Allegra Kent*

To enjoy the task of learning how to dance the Argentine tango, you need to get in shape—in tango shape, that is. You will learn about how to manage your body in terms of balance, motion, and posture. This chapter presents the tools you need for successfully stepping onto the dance floor with anybody, anywhere, anytime. With clearly indicated exceptions, these tools are equally important for both men and women. Incorporating new body mechanics as an adult is likely to present challenges to both the brain and body. These new mechanics may not make much sense in your daily life and may go against everything you learned at an early age to keep you from tripping, falling, and looking silly when you walk. Therefore, you will switch your brain to "manual" and refrain from mentally interfering during the process in which you teach your body new ways to stay balanced and to move and be moved.

TANGO BARRE, A FITNESS PROGRAM FOR TANGO DANCERS

Anyone who uses movement for expression knows that the fundamental skills are the tools used for a lifetime in the pursuit of effective movement. Fundamentals are not to be discarded during the passage from a beginning to an accomplished product—that is, you, the seasoned dancer. The more you use and practice the things you learn in this program, the more confidence you will have and the more substance your dancing will have. As you begin to execute the various movements presented in this chapter, you might find that your body is a bit tense and not prepared for the flexibility required for dancing tango. You can do many exercises to help you incorporate this unique way of walking the tango into your body memory. Here are some exercises you can use frequently to keep you tango fit.

The Shape of Your Feet and the Look of Your Legs

Watch this demonstrated on the DVD

Stand with your feet together, upper thighs gently in contact with each other, and your weight on the balls of your feet. Rotate your feet outward. Your feet will touch heel to heel, with your toes pointing outward. The shape of your two feet forms a V. Place your hand on the front of your hip muscle. Turn your feet in so that they completely touch each other; then turn them out. You should feel that when your feet turn out, your hips open. Optimal range of motion is achieved when the hips are opened. The span of the V at this stage of your training should be 10 o'clock for the left foot and 2 o'clock for the right foot. Once the body internalizes the separation and the feet are opened naturally, the opening may vary according to your own preferences, as long as there is a distinct V shape with heels touching.

The three fundamental opening movements with each leg are forward, side, and back. These are generated from the hips. Play a tango with a moderate tempo, and keep time to the tempo as you do this exercise. Do the sequence using all three positions: front, then side, then back. Stand on one leg in the neutral position. Extend the other leg forward, and then bring it back. Extend the leg to the side, and then bring it back to neutral. And finally, extend the leg back, and then bring it to neutral.

1. Shift your weight completely to the left leg so that your body rests comfortably on it. This is called being on axis.

2. Extend the right (free) leg forward using the base of your little toe to make the first contact with the floor. Keep your heel facing down to the floor. See figure 3.1a.

3. Bring the right leg back to the starting position (to "neutral," or "home"). This is your resting position on axis, the finishing position of any step. Your inner thighs and heels should gently press against each other. The toes should be pointed outward to solidify your base of support.

4. From the resting position, extend your right leg to the side (lateral opening). Curl up the big toe and touch the ground with the inside edge of the foot. Keep your heel facing the floor. See figure 3.1b.

5. Return your right leg to the resting position as in step 3.

6. From the resting position, open the right leg straight to your back using the same foot placement as in step 4. Curl up and use the front edge of your big toe. See figure 3.1c.

7. Return your right leg to the resting position as in step 3.

8. Change your axis to the right leg and repeat steps 1 through 7 using the left leg.

Figure 3.1 Foot placement for *(a)* forward, *(b)* side, and *(c)* back step.

Disassociation of Upper and Lower Body

Flexibility and separation between the upper and lower body are physical skills you need to have in order to move fluently in the tango.

1. Sit down in a chair.
2. Keep your legs in an open, relaxed position, with your feet turned out.
3. Rest your right arm on the back of the chair.
4. While keeping your lower body facing forward, bring your left arm to the right arm, and turn your body toward the back of the chair.
5. Repeat this four times.

Do this for the other side of your body, too, with your left arm resting on the back of the chair and your right arm turning toward the back of the chair.

Now stand up. Mind your foot placement. Repeat the following exercise eight times:

1. Place your weight on the left leg, and step forward with the right leg.
2. Now wrap your arms around your shoulders (hug yourself).
3. Bend your forward knee gently, and turn your entire torso into the direction of your forward leg.
4. Return to the starting position.

Try to keep the heel of your back leg on the floor. Switch legs and do this exercise for the other side of your body: Standing on your right leg, step forward with the left leg and turn your upper torso to the left. Although partners spend more time to the right of each other, in tango the partner can either be to your right or to your left. You turn left and right to acknowledge the partner's presence, so you must develop symmetrical flexibility.

This is such an important concept that it deserves to be spelled out as one of the fundamental tenets of tango: The dance is circular by nature, and you must be able to navigate the crowded floors of the dance halls. The woman moving blindly against a crowd of similar-minded people must always dance with the intention of surrounding the man left to right or right to left as guided by the man, never pedaling back away from him or charging into him. The man may surround the woman at times, but most important, he must dance around the floor.

Tango dancers don't travel with their feet on parallel tracks facing each other (leading and following). They travel with both feet on one track, whether they share the same track or are on different tracks. That way they are always right or left of each other, trading places or changing tracks as they dance. Forward, side, and back steps always need to be done with the intention of surrounding one's partner, even when they both move in what appears to be (but is not) a straight line. Both men and women must dance to their partners.

FIRST FIND YOUR AXIS

The axis is the vertical line formed by the head, shoulder, hip, knee, and foot, which means that the axis can be on the right or the left side of the body, as the weight is transferred to either side. In other words, when you find your axis, you'll be standing with your entire body weight on one leg. To improve the equilibrium while balanced on one leg, you must elongate the upper body, and the other hip must be relaxed so that the leg attached to it hangs loose and ready to swing from the hip in any direction.

Favoring either leg on your axis grounds the hip on which your weight is resting in such a way that the only possible motion for that hip is circular. The circular motion is the result of your upper body rotating enough so that it eventually makes the hip turn, which in turn forces the foot on which you are standing to pivot. Pivoting has the main purpose of pointing the grounded hip into a different direction. This is an important concept to understand since the embrace does not allow the upper body to fully turn. Therefore, the connection between the upper body and the hips must be fluid so that the plane of both parts of the body can be broken—thus the commonly used term *quebrada*, which literally means "broken," as is the line between the upper body and the hips.

quebrada—*Break; broken. A posture in which the body breaks at the waist and uses a deep bend of the knees.*

We have thought many times that the phrase "Got Axis?" deserves to be emblazoned on T-shirts for tango dancers because it carries an important message: Are you capable of holding yourself balanced with your entire body weight resting on one leg? If you have waited in line at the post office, the checkout counter at the supermarket, or anywhere where you must spend long periods standing up without moving, you already know the basic skill of resting your body on one leg or taking the load off the other leg, or being on axis. As your legs get tired, your brain makes your body rest on one leg while taking the load off the other. As time passes and the leg holding the body's weight gets tired, the brain makes the body rest on the other leg, allowing the initial leg to get a deserved rest. All of that happens without your direct intervention.

The concept of axis in tango has the same fundamental purpose: to rest the weight of your body on one leg while taking the load off the other. The underlying difference here is that instead of sinking or sitting on the load-bearing leg, you will stand up on the load-bearing leg and elongate your body. To elongate, you will take a deep breath, feeling the sensation that you are on top of your feet or on the highest step of a staircase or on top of a pedestal. As you elongate upward on the support (load-bearing) leg, the free leg will naturally hang with your upper thighs and heels touching. To properly present the axis to your partner, place the instep of the free foot against the back of the heel of the axis-bearing foot. To make sure you understand how to do it, stand up and read this paragraph five times while making axis on the left leg. Take a deep breath and make yourself very tall so that there is room for the right leg to dangle from the hip in a closed-thigh position. Change your weight to the right leg and read this paragraph again five times, repeating the exercise.

Each dancer has two axes, a right axis and a left axis. The simplest way to describe movement in tango is by describing the act of changing axis—in place or to any point within a circular area around the support leg. So your first goal is to develop an axis and then to change it in a controlled way. Individually, you will have to exert some action on your body to change axis. In an actual dancing situation, the man will be responsible for changing his own and his partner's axis. The woman will be responsible for acquiring a stable, relaxed, balanced posture once she has been placed on one of her axes.

Changing Axis to the Beat of a Tango

Stand up straight with shoulders relaxed and both heels together in the V position. Place your weight on the ball (metatarsal) of the foot rather than on the heel. Raise both arms and pretend you are hugging somebody.

Watch this demonstrated on the DVD

Take a deep breath and gently transfer your weight to the left leg by slightly raising the right heel and gently bending the right knee while exhaling. Inhale again and transfer your weight to the right leg by slightly raising the left heel and gently bending the left knee while exhaling. Do this four times, then relax and repeat the entire sequence as many times as you need in order to change axis in a natural way. Once you are comfortable changing axis in place, play some tango music and time your weight changes to the beat of the piece you are listening to.

The Center of Your Domain

The place where you are standing on axis at any given time is the center of an imaginary circle, which you carry with you as you move in any direction. In any instance, wherever you land at the end of a step, as you look straight ahead (your north), the half circle that lies to your left constitutes your left, or west, side. Any leg action that will favor your weight in that space would be considered a move to your left. Similarly, the half circle that lies to your right constitutes your right, or east, side, and any leg action that will favor your weight in that space would be considered a move to your right.

The half circle in front of your chest is your forward, or north, space, and the half circle behind your back is your backward, or south, space. As you learn about motion and trajectories in tango, it is important that you understand and identify the space you move to as one of four quadrants with respect to where you start from: forward right, forward left, backward right, and backward left (see figure 3.2). This demarcation of space with regard to the initial starting spot of every step is extremely critical. It helps you understand the circular nature of the dance and become acquainted with an important concept of the tango: The man makes the woman dance around him as he dances around the floor. Therefore, your partner will either be in your right or your left quadrant, never in front, and of course never behind.

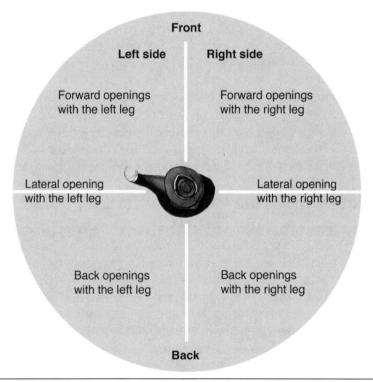

Figure 3.2 The infinite possibilities for moving from the instant position into four quadrants using openings.

Reaching Out

Now you will learn about the six root motions of the legs when dancing the tango. Don't forget to breathe normally while you do these exercises. Keep your arms in an embrace shape and assume the proper placement of the feet. See figures 3.3 and 3.4 for demonstrations of the steps.

Watch this demonstrated on the DVD

1. Stand on your right axis.

2. Bend the right knee slightly, and begin to extend the left foot to your left side from the hip. Keep contact with the floor with the base of the big toe until the leg is completely extended. This is called a lateral opening to the left.

3. Straighten the right knee and let the left leg close until the upper thighs are touching and your feet are in a V shape.

4. Change your axis to the left leg. Bend the left knee slightly, and extend the right foot to the side from the hip. Keep contact with the floor with the base of the big toe until the leg is completely extended. This is called a lateral opening to the right. Straighten the left knee and let the right leg close until the upper thighs are touching and your feet are in a V shape.

5. Change your axis to the right leg.

6. Bend the right knee slightly, and extend the left leg backward from the hip, keeping the foot pointing in the 10 o'clock position. Keep contact with the floor with the base of the big toe curled up until the leg is completely extended. This is called a backward opening on the left side.

7. Straighten the right knee and let the left leg close until the thighs are touching, keeping your feet in a V shape.

8. Change your axis to the left leg. Bend the left knee slightly, and extend the right leg backward from the hip, keeping the foot pointing in the 2 o'clock position. Keep contact with the floor with the base of the big toe curled up until the leg is completely extended. This is called a backward opening on the right side.

9. Straighten the left knee and let the right leg close until the upper thighs are touching, keeping your feet in a V shape.

10. Change your axis to the right leg.

11. Bend the right knee slightly, and extend the left leg forward from the hip. Keep contact with the floor with the base of the little toe pointing in the 10 o'clock position until the left leg is completely extended. This is called a forward opening on the left.

12. Straighten the right knee and let the left leg close until the upper thighs are touching and your feet are in a V shape.

13. Change your axis to the left leg. Bend the left knee slightly, and extend the right leg forward from the hip. Keep contact with the floor with the base of the little toe pointing in the 2 o'clock position until the leg is completely straight. This is called a forward opening on the right.

14. Straighten the left knee and let the right leg close until the upper thighs are touching and your feet are in a V shape.

Figure 3.3 The six root motions of the leg from the woman's point of view: *(a)* lateral opening to the left, *(b)* back opening to the left, *(c)* forward opening to the left, *(d)* lateral opening to the right, *(e)* back opening to the right, and *(f)* forward opening to the right.

Figure 3.4 The six root motions of the leg from the man's point of view: *(a)* lateral opening to the left, *(b)* back opening to the left, *(c)* forward opening to the left, *(d)* lateral opening to the right, *(e)* back opening to the right, and *(f)* forward opening to the right.

ANATOMY OF A STEP

You now know how to establish an axis and reach in the three main directions from the center of your domain. You will now learn how to change axis in six different ways, or how to "make steps." The fundamental mechanics of moving by changing axis are the same regardless of direction, and they define what we call the anatomy of a step.

To begin a step, you'll stand on axis, bearing the weight of your body on one leg so the other leg is free to reach into the direction of the step. To finish a step, you will change axis to the other leg.

Tips for Tango Technique

1. Bend the load-bearing knee, bringing your body downward.

2. Extend the free leg down to the floor, pushing it in such a way as to caress the floor with the base of the big toe (lateral or backward steps) or the base of the little toe (forward step).

3. For side and back steps, curl up your big toe so that the foot and ankle can bend. This creates a foot position that is called the "broken ankle."

4. Do not use the point of the toe, but rather the side, the edge of the entire base of the big toe, touching the floor with the entire side of the foot.

5. For forward steps, use the entire base of the little toe as the first contact with the floor. Do not point the toe. Again, curl up the big toe and keep your heel facing down to the floor.

6. Remember to turn your toes out. Do not dance with your feet straight together, or worse yet, turned in.

7. The more you bend the support knee, the farther the free leg will reach in full extension.

8. Elongate the calf of the free leg so that the ball of the foot presses against the floor.

9. Push gently with the support leg to transfer your body weight to the new axis. Elongate the calf to drop the heel of the free leg.

10. As the free leg becomes the support leg, let the knee bend naturally to receive the weight transfer. Straighten the knee to allow the other leg to come to the resting position with upper thighs touching and heels together.

In summary, there are three components to each tango step. The first one is the placement of the toe. The second involves rolling onto the ball of the foot. The third requires the dropping of the heel to the ground to receive the full weight of the body.

Steps are classified into three categories: openings, inside crosses, and outside crosses. They can be executed on a clockwise and counterclockwise trajectory for a total of six fundamental movements of the legs. Simply put, in tango we will always use one of these six fundamental movements to define, describe, and execute every pattern. So, it is important that you learn to identify each step as being one of these six fundamental movements. Remember that when you dance, your partner will be either to your left or to your right. When partners are to the right of each other, a forward motion of the right leg is considered an inside cross to the right because from the vantage point of your partner, your right leg seems to be crossed in front of or inside the left leg. Similarly, a back motion of the left leg is considered an outside cross to the left because from your partner's point of view, the left leg appears as if it is crossed behind or outside the right leg.

When partners are to the left of each other, a forward motion of the left leg is considered an inside cross to the left because from the vantage point of your partner, your left leg seems to be crossed in front or inside the right leg. Similarly, a back motion of the right leg is considered an outside cross to the right because from your partner's point of view, the right leg appears as if it is crossed behind or outside the left leg.

The remaining two fundamental movements are openings, one with the right leg and one with the left leg. Except at the beginning of the dance when the dancers choose to start with a lateral opening (side step), all lateral openings follow crosses if moving in the same direction, or another lateral opening if changing directions. You will find it helpful to review this section later on when you have begun to study turns and changes of directions. For now, try to understand the logic of what follows. When your partner is to your right, a forward motion of the left leg becomes an opening because the leg is outside from your partner's point of view. When your partner is to your left, a forward motion of the right leg becomes an opening because the leg is outside from your partner's point of view. Similarly, when your partner is to your right, a back motion of the right leg becomes an opening to the left, the degree of which is determined by whether your partner is moving in the same direction as you are. Finally, when your partner is to your left, a back motion of the left leg becomes an opening to the right, the degree of which is determined by whether your partner is moving in the same direction as you are.

The most important concept here, and one that has a profound effect in understanding the structure of the Argentine tango dance, is that side steps in their geometric definition do not exist. You will learn that what your eyes see is not what is really happening. Tango dancers create many illusions that the casual observer may try to imitate with disastrous results. As you dance with an understanding of structure and mechanics, watching yourself on a video will surprise you because you create an illusion for the spectator. When you dance, you must remember where the center of your domain is and how your coordinates change instantaneously as you move. As you dance with the intention of surrounding your partner, if you take two forward steps, one will be an inside cross and the next one an opening. Similarly, if you take two back steps, one will be an outside cross and the next one an opening. The illusion of a side step is created by the rotation of the body as you take the next step following a cross with the intention of surrounding your partner. The same thing happens if you take a forward step with the inside leg and allow your upper body to turn with the intention of surrounding your partner. You will have created the illusion of crossed legs.

Inside Cross to the Right

Watch this demonstrated on the DVD

The following exercise requires that you walk forward in a circular clockwise trajectory assuming that your partner is to your right (see figure 3.5a). Extend your right hand in front of you as if your hand is your partner.

1. Stand on your left axis.

2. Begin turning your upper body to your right as you bend your left leg. At the same time extend the right leg forward in the direction of your hand.

3. Keep turning your upper body until you feel that both thighs are firmly pressed together.

4. Complete the forward step by transferring your weight completely to your right axis and presenting a new axis to your partner.

Inside Cross to the Left

Watch this demonstrated on the DVD

The following exercise requires that you walk forward in a circular counterclockwise trajectory assuming that your partner is to your left (see figure 3.5b). Extend your left hand in front of you as if your hand is your partner.

1. Stand on your right axis.

2. Begin turning your upper body to your left as you bend your right leg. At the same time extend the left leg forward in the direction of your hand.

3. Keep turning your upper body until you feel that both thighs are firmly pressed together.

4. Complete the forward step by transferring your weight completely to your left axis and presenting a new axis to your partner.

Figure 3.5 Inside forward cross (*a*) to the right and (*b*) to the left.

Outside Cross to the Right

The following exercise requires that you walk backward in a circular clock-wise trajectory assuming that your partner is to your left (see figure 3.6a). Extend your left hand in front of you as if your hand is your partner.

Watch this demonstrated on the DVD

1. Stand on your left axis.
2. Bend your left leg and begin turning your upper body to your left at the same time that you extend the right leg backward in the direction of your hand.
3. Keep turning your upper body until you feel that both thighs are firmly pressed together.
4. Complete the back step by transferring your weight completely to your right leg, presenting a new axis to your partner.

Outside Cross to the Left

The following exercise requires that you walk backward in a circular counterclockwise trajectory assuming that your partner is to your right (see figure 3.6b). Extend your right hand in front of you as if your hand is your partner.

Watch this demonstrated on the DVD

1. Stand on your right axis.
2. Begin turning your upper body to your right. Bend your right leg and at the same time extend the left leg backward in the direction of your hand.
3. Keep turning your upper body until you feel that both thighs are firmly pressed together.
4. Complete the back step by transferring your weight completely to your left leg, presenting a new axis to your partner.

Figure 3.6 Outside back cross *(a)* to the right and *(b)* to the left.

Openings

An opening is any movement that separates the upper thighs in order to allow the free leg to reach another position. There are three kinds of openings: one that follows a forward inside cross, one that follows a back outside cross, and one that follows another opening when changing directions. When using openings (laterals or side steps) to change direction, whoever opens to the left will do so with a *long* step and whoever opens to the right will do so with a *short* opening. A *long* opening extends beyond the width of the shoulders; a *short* opening is about shoulder's length. Openings can be either to the right or to the left of the center of your domain.

To execute an opening to the right, do the following:

1. Stand up on your left axis and bend the knee.
2. From the hip, curl up the right big toe, and extend the right leg down to the floor laterally, sweeping away with the base of the big toe.
3. Elongate your left knee to push your weight first over the ball and then over the heel of the right foot.
4. Elongate your right knee, and bring your body up to allow the left leg to close, presenting a new axis.

To execute an opening to the left, do the following:

1. Stand up on your right axis and bend the knee.
2. From the hip, extend the left leg down to the floor laterally, sweeping away with the base of the curled-up big toe.
3. Elongate the right knee to push your weight first over the ball and then over the heel of the left foot.
4. Elongate your left knee, and bring your body up to allow the right leg to close, presenting a new axis.

You have now learned how to create the six fundamental steps of the tango, taking into consideration that your partner always is to your right or to your left. It is time to begin linking different combinations of these six steps to define predictable trajectories that allow you and your partner to glide around the floor, respecting the flow of the dance.

RESOLUTION

Watch this demonstrated on the DVD

The term *resolution* refers to the action of resolving, ending, finishing, and taking care of business. In tango it is used to end a sequence much the same way as a period is used to end a sentence.

A resolution is a very simple yet understated and elegant way for the couple to gently turn around the floor. There is a forward resolution with its matching backward resolution (see figure 3.7), and there is a resolution to the right with its mirror resolution to the left.

For a forward resolution to the right or tango close, do the following:

1. Stand on your right axis.
2. Advance forward with your left leg while turning your upper body to your left (inside cross).
3. Advance forward in a circular trajectory with your right leg until the two feet come together.
4. Without stopping, pass the right leg and extend it from the hip down to the floor laterally, sweeping away with the base of the curled-up right big toe (*long* lateral opening).
5. Transfer your weight to the right leg and bring it and the left leg together. Switch axis in place (close).
6. Step back on a diagonal to your right.
7. Repeat four times.

For a backward resolution to the left or tango close, do the following:

1. Stand on your left axis.
2. Step back on a diagonal with your right leg while turning your upper body to your left.
3. Step back in a circular trajectory with your left leg until the two feet come together.
4. Without stopping, pass the left leg and extend it from the hip down to the floor laterally, sweeping away with the base of the curled-up left big toe (*long* lateral opening).
5. Transfer your weight to the left leg and bring it and the right leg together. Switch axis in place (close).
6. Step forward with your left leg to change axis.
7. Repeat four times.

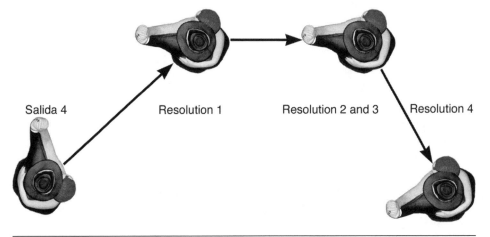

Salida 4   Resolution 1   Resolution 2 and 3   Resolution 4

Figure 3.7 Trajectory of a resolution to the right.

CHANGE OF FRONT

Watch this demonstrated on the DVD

We define a change of front (*cambio de frente*) as a three-step sequence in which the dancer ends up facing in the opposite direction from where he or she started. In other words, a change of front is defined as either a sequence beginning with an inside cross (forward) followed by an opening and ending with an outside cross (backward), or a sequence beginning with an outside cross (backward) followed by an opening and ending with an inside cross (forward). Changes of front can be either to the right or to the left (see figure 3.8).

For a forward-to-back change of front to the right, do the following:

1. Stand on your left axis.
2. Execute an inside cross with your right leg while turning to your right.
3. Execute an opening to the left with your left leg.
4. Execute an outside cross with your right leg.

For a backward-to-front change of front to the right, do the following:

1. Stand on your right axis.
2. Execute an outside cross with your left leg.
3. Execute an opening to the right with your right leg.
4. Execute an inside cross with your left leg.

For forward-to-back change of front to the left, do the following:

1. Stand on your right axis.
2. Execute an inside cross with your left leg while turning to your left.
3. Execute an opening to the right with your right leg.
4. Execute an outside cross with your left leg.

For a backward-to-front change of front to the left, do the following:

1. Stand on your left axis.
2. Execute an outside cross with your right leg.
3. Execute an opening to the left with your left leg.
4. Execute an inside cross with your right leg.

As a general rule, an opening links each cross. If after the second cross you add a second opening, you are back where you started. You can repeat the same change of front again, completing a full circle. The importance of the change of front will become obvious as you use two consecutive changes of front to learn a fundamental piece of navigation that we call *la base* (BAH-say).

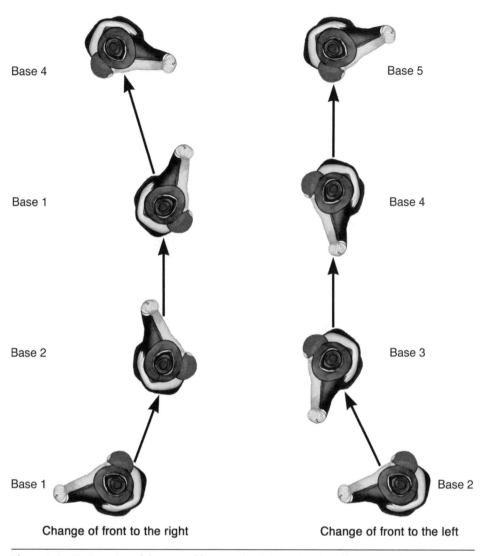

Figure 3.8 Trajectories of changes of front to the right and to the left.

LA BASE

The entire sequence consists of six steps: two lateral openings, two forward steps, and two back steps. La base is a valuable tool because it uses the six steps of the tango while creating a stationary rectangular pattern. You will need a space large enough for you to walk forward and backward at least three steps. The simple definition of la base is as follows:

> Watch this demonstrated on the DVD

1. Execute a forward-to-back change of front to the left.
2. Execute a backward-to-front change of front to the left.
3. Repeat.

Let's break it down so you can understand the structure of the pattern. For the purpose of practicing only, you will first use a box in the shape of a parallelogram (see figure 3.9). When going forward, you will use a diagonal to your left; when moving backward, you will use a diagonal to your right. Your partner will always be on your right, so extend your right arm to indicate that.

1. Open (long) to the left with your left leg.
2. Step forward with your right leg, placing your right foot in front of your left foot.
3. Step forward with your left leg, moving your left foot in a straight line.
4. Open (short) to the right with your right leg.
5. Step back with your left leg, placing it in-line behind your right foot.
6. Step back with your right leg, on a diagonal to your right.
7. Repeat steps 1 through 6 eight times, minding your weight changes and feet placement and always dancing to your right hand.

Once your body has internalized the sequence (side-forward-forward-side-back-back), it's time to remember that side steps as geometric entities do not exist. What are commonly referred to as side steps are actually openings that follow crosses if moving in the same direction or follow another lateral opening

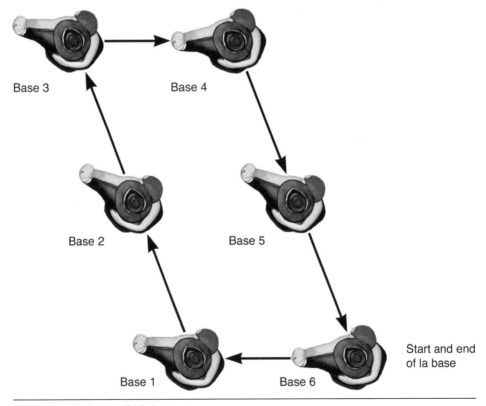

Base 3   Base 4

Base 2   Base 5

Start and end
of la base

Base 1   Base 6

Figure 3.9 Trajectory for la base.

if changing directions. Since your partner will be to your right when you do la base, the first forward step is always with the right leg (an inside forward cross). The second forward step is always with the left leg, and it is actually a forward opening. The opening following the second forward step is another forward motion of the right leg, with a rotation of the upper body to the left. The first back step is always with the left leg, and it is an outside back cross. The second back step is an inside diagonal back opening. The opening following the second back step is another backward motion of the leg, with a rotation of the upper body to the left, resulting in a long opening to the left. With careful management of the angle that you use to turn for the lateral openings, you'll begin to move around the dance floor in a counterclockwise fashion (or, in shorthand, following the line of dance). Openings are an effective tool for the man to use in steering the couple around the floor in an orderly fashion. Openings allow the woman to readjust her position in relation to the man's shoulders to make sure she is always right or left of him.

THE CODE OF THE TANGO

The code of the tango defines the way the woman will walk surrounding the man according to a predictable and repetitive sequence. That sequence uses inside crosses and outside crosses linked by openings as she progresses in either a clockwise or counterclockwise circular trajectory around the man. When turning to the right of the man, the woman will use her right leg to cross inside and outside, and she will use her left leg to open, using three of the six fundamental steps (see figure 3.10). When turning to the left of the man, the woman will use her left leg to cross inside and outside, and she will use her right leg to open, using the remaining three of the six fundamental steps.

Figure 3.10 The code of the tango: *(a)* inside forward cross, *(b)* opening, and *(c)* outside back cross.

The code is a sequence designed to allow the woman to surround the man while dancing. There are instances in which the man will make use of elements of the code to complement the motion of the woman and to create complex patterns. But for the purpose of defining roles, the code is primarily a mantra for the woman that ensures a predictable way to dance to the right or left side of the man. All dancers, regardless of gender, must understand the code, be proficient in its execution, and use it according to their roles. In typical fashion, the man will indicate the trajectory of the woman and mark the inside and outside crosses as he sends her around him. The woman will walk around the man, observing the progressive sequence of her legs to execute the code.

The code is activated as soon as the woman moves a second step in the same direction (that is, either to the right or to the left of the man). The resulting trajectory looks different depending on whether the man is stationary in one position or moving forward or backward. The definition of the code, however, is the same in all cases: Alternate inside front and outside back crosses linked by openings. The opening leg is always the one favoring or leading into the direction of the movement. The crossing leg is the one opposite the direction of the movement. Simply put, when the woman moves into the left side of the man (her right), she opens with her right leg and crosses with her left leg. When the woman moves into the right side of the man (her left), she opens with her left leg and crosses with her right leg.

A typical application of the code of the tango is a trajectory that follows a diagonal into the southeast quadrant (backward to the right). Extend your right arm to indicate the position of your partner to your right.

Watch this demonstrated on the DVD

1. Stand up straight with your axis on your left leg.
2. Open (short) laterally to your right with your right leg and change axis.
3. Step back on a diagonal to your right with your left leg using an outside back cross, turning your upper body gently to your right.
4. Step back opening your right leg on the same diagonal to your right and change axis, allowing your body to stop traveling.
5. Swivel your right hip gently to the left and pull the left leg to cross in front of the right leg. Keep your weight on the balls of your feet with your heels on the ground. Change your axis to your left leg by gently bending both knees, allowing the right kneecap to push firmly into the back of the left knee.

At this point your legs should be locked, your heels firmly on the floor, and your body balanced and comfortable. Next, elongate your upper torso, take a deep breath, and place your weight completely on the left leg. As the knees straighten, the right leg will be freed. Repeat the four-step pattern four times.

To develop a natural way to move and respond to the music, make tango fitness exercises a part of your daily routine. As an individual, you will always hold yourself in a balanced position and then send your body in the direction you want to move. This will force you to "fall" off your axis and use the free leg to receive the transfer of your body weight to the next position, where you will assume a new axis and a new balanced position.

With a partner, you must know how to move the other, and you must know how to be moved. You can alternate roles as an exercise or you can hone the particular skills for each role. In either case, the man moves and holds the woman on axis as he moves and holds himself on axis. The woman maintains an axis and allows herself to be moved from axis to axis.

Since most of the dancing is done with your partner to the right, you must be aware of established conventions within the structure of the dance.

1. The first forward step is always an inside cross with the right leg.
2. The second forward step is always an opening with the left leg.
3. The first back step is always an outside cross with the left leg.
4. The second back step is always a diagonal opening with the right leg.
5. Side steps or lateral openings to the left are "long."
6. Side steps or lateral openings to the right are "short."
7. The woman dances around the man.
8. The man dances around the floor.

The material in this chapter contains the set of basic tools that both men and women will need in order to dance together. We can't stress enough the importance of exercising, practicing, and developing the skills to use these tools to your benefit.

CHAPTER 4

To Hug or Not to Hug

The tango is so intimate that one gets confused: you fall in love
with the tango and you fall in love with the tango dancer.

—*Vanina Bilous, professional dancer and teacher*

The most unique characteristic of the Argentine tango is the embrace
(el abrazo). Many social dances involve the couple holding each other,
and points of contact are the arms and hands. Some postures are
idealized, as in some ballroom dances. Some postures have the couple loosely
connected. Most dances, with the exception of the Argentine tango, allow both
partners to have total control of their movements. These dances are based
on the concept of one person leading and the other person following. That
requires memorizing patterns in order to match the mechanical execution of
both the leader's steps and the follower's steps.

Symbolically, the embrace of the tango, el abrazo, represents deeply longed-
for human contact and connection. The Argentine tango is rooted in the
philosophy of embracing another
human being. As the tango has
evolved, its posture of the embrace
has remained instantly recognizable
and respected by generation after

> **abrazo**—*Embrace. The tango hug.*

generation of tango dancers in Argentina. However, the fundamental purpose
of the embrace has been diluted as the dance has reached across borders and
become a global pastime.

In the new millennium there is some discussion and confusion about the
different styles of embracing a partner in the Argentine tango. The embrace
has erroneously been called "open" or "closed," depending on whom you
are dancing with, where you are dancing, and even what rhythm you are
dancing to. Tango for export, openly loathed by the social dancers in Buenos
Aires, has made a big impression on people outside Argentina. Show tango,
with its acrobatic jumps, exaggerated flying legs, and extreme stereotyping
of men and women, was the first imagery that caught people's attention
and fed into the naïve belief that anybody could do that in a social setting.
Gradually, the social dancing of the *milongueros*, the regulars at the Buenos

Aires dance halls, began to transcend borders giving tango dancing an entire new framework. Devoid of the traditions, culture, and codes of the milongueros, idiosyncratic mannerisms and affectations have been packaged into a so-called close-embrace, milonguero-style, in which people are encouraged to imitate each other with preordained patterns and elitist behavior. Since the essence of tango is sheer improvisation, freedom to improvise is a hallmark of open minds. Style follows technique, and good dancers develop a personal style after acquiring solid technique. What identifies people as tango dancers is the unique way they dance Argentine tango: with a higher-than-average degree of closeness. Tango is the ultimate contact dance. The main purpose of the embrace is to establish points of contact between the partners.

When viewed within the historical context of the formation of the dance, space was and is scarce in the dance halls of Buenos Aires. The look of the dance today is a direct result of the environment in which it was developed. When dancing, it is helpful to hold the image of yourself as part of a couple carrying your own personal space around a very crowded dance floor. The couple is contained in a space that has the shape of a cylinder. Another metaphor is imagining that you're dancing on one moving tile of a tiled dance floor. Unless you dance in an urban place where there are hundreds of couples sharing the floor, it is difficult to imagine the need to dance close and only in the space your two bodies occupy. If you want the authentic look of the Argentine tango as it is danced in Buenos Aires, you should accept these images, even if you are the only couple on the dance floor.

The posture of tango is formed by the image of a hug. When you see someone and greet that person with a hug, be aware of the position of your own arms and the other person's arms. We don't hug by pulling our heads away from each other, throwing our shoulders back, and offering a rigid frame of arms with elbows sticking out at right angles. Rather, our heads and faces touch, our arms are relaxed, our elbows are down near the waist, and our shoulders are softened. There is nothing rigid in our posture.

ANATOMY OF THE EMBRACE

Watch this demonstrated on the DVD

You begin by facing your partner. If one is not available at this time, use your imagination and proceed to learn the anatomy of the embrace from your gender's point of view. The woman has to stand up with the weight on the balls of her feet, the heels on the ground and touching, and the feet opened in a V shape. She should wait for the man to approach, keeping her body from shadowing his. She needs to open her left arm slightly away from her body to make room for the man's initial reach with his right arm. The man also needs to stand up correctly in front of his partner. The V of his feet should be centered on her left foot to facilitate the process of embracing his partner.

1. Relax your shoulders and keep your elbows down.

2. Man: Extend your right arm forward and straight down until the inside of your forearm makes contact with the side of your partner's body, regardless of her height.

3. Man: Bend your lower (right) arm from the elbow and encircle your partner just above her waist, loosening your shoulder to reach without bending.

4. Man: Adjust for the woman's height by raising or lowering your lower arm from the elbow so that your right hand can come to rest horizontally at the middle of her back. Keep your fingers relaxed and closed.

5. Woman: Once your partner has embraced you with his right arm, loosen up your left shoulder, reach forward, and raise your left arm.

6. Woman: Place the inside portion of the triceps of your left upper arm firmly against any part of the man's encircling arm.

7. Man: Raise your upper left arm to your left. Point your lower left arm up toward your partner, to form a V shape. Keep your elbow bent and pointing down.

8. Man: Twist your left wrist to open your left hand facing up and out.

9. Woman: Extend your right arm forward and up to form a V with your elbow pointing down. Rest your right palm down on the gentleman's palm.

10. Man: Close your fingers around the lady's hand gently, and slightly turn your wrist inward to create a slight tension between your palm and your partner's palm.

11. This is not a handshake but a soft connection. There should be no squeezing or gripping. Do not use the open side of the embrace for balance or to avoid falling off axis! See figure 4.1.

Figure 4.1 The woman extends her right arm forward and up to form a V with her elbow pointing down. She rests her right palm on the man's palm.

If the embrace is approached in this fashion, any subtle motion of the man's upper body will be felt very clearly by the woman, and her upper body will move accordingly. Since feet follow the body, dynamic interactions of the

Figure 4.2 The woman places the inside portion of her triceps firmly against any part of the man's encircling arm.

upper bodies result in a visually pleasant and smooth displacement of the dancing couple. There should never be any space between the man's right arm and the woman's left arm (see figure 4.2). It is the woman who determines what is close enough. If need be, the woman can scoop her hand under the man's biceps and hold it like a small pocketbook. She can also rest her left hand on the man's shoulder or upper arm or even behind his neck. The hand must be relaxed, with the fingers closed (please, no clawlike or karate-chop hands). There shouldn't be any tension in the hand placed on the man's body. The man should barely be aware of the woman's left hand.

The man should never use his left arm as a pump to force motion on his partner. If the man pushes with his left arm, he will cause the woman to lose control of her axis. In turn, the woman will try to regain her balance by pushing or hanging with her right arm. Dancers who are technically challenged are notorious for using the open side of the embrace for arm wrestling. The woman's right shoulder should never get behind her body. The man will learn to guide his partner using his right arm, extending it to separate from her and contracting it to come closer to her. To make her move laterally to his right side, the man will open his right shoulder. To make her move laterally to his left side, the man will move his right shoulder across his body to his left.

As a couple, act as if there is no space to either side of you. Don't raise your elbows and let them stick out, because you might poke someone in the eye as you turn. Dancers shouldn't infringe on the space of other dancers. Practice relaxing your shoulders, which will help you keep your elbows down. This also enhances the points of contact between partners and facilitates better communication via body language.

Finally, notice that the embrace is fully closed on the man's right side (the woman's left side). On the other side, with both arms extended in a W shape, the embrace is slightly more open. This causes the couple's bodies to form a gentle V-shaped frame. The angle of the V shape is totally optional and decided mutually by the dancers. There is no prescribed angle for the V shape. It can be anywhere from 0 to almost 45 degrees. As a minimum requirement, the left side of the woman's upper body should rest gently against the center of the man's chest.

Head Position and Direction of Gaze

When dancing tango, each partner must maintain his or her own axis, establishing points of contact through the embrace, so neither cheeks nor heads can have continuous contact. There is a misconception that may lead some tango dancers to want to dance "cheek to cheek." Again, please keep in mind that the embrace is fluid. If heads and cheeks are plastered against each other, there is no room to move within a flexible embrace. If you persist in adhering to a mistaken image, you will limit movement. An unfortunate result for the woman is the ungainly line of her rear end sticking out.

The heads of both partners should be level and relaxed. The woman must always maintain visual connection with her partner's body. In the Argentine tango the woman must be able to respond in the "now." There is no time to analyze cues, recognize "leads," and decide how to follow, because the man needs to improvise to navigate the dance floor. His partner must dance

Figure 4.3 Good counter body position.

with him in the moment, not after the fact. So in addition to physical cues from the man that constitute the skill of *la marca* (the physical marking or indicating of the woman's movements by the man), the woman can use many visual cues by always looking at where the man's body is, where it is going, and when it is stopping. She can see the space he is proposing she move into. She can only peripherally see in front of her. She must always look toward his torso, either through his right or his left shoulder. Each one of the partners in the couple must be focused into the embrace, not away from it. Even if you adopt a position of heads being counter to one another (that is, the woman looking over the right shoulder of the man), we suggest that the woman direct her vision to her right side (his left side) by simply looking that way (see figure 4.3). The slightest intention is of value.

The man needs to look around at the dance floor, of course, since he is responsible for navigating the floor. However, he must not forget to make visual contact with his partner, too. In general, where the head goes the body follows. So if you make a turn or a movement to your left, you'll look to the left. If you go to your right, look in that direction. There is nothing more unsettling and contrary to the essence of the tango for either partner than when one feels that the other one never looks their way. Dance to your partner, not to the space.

The man needs to see where he is placing the woman. The woman needs to see where his body is taking her, and then go there. This continuous cooperation and interaction between the two give the Argentine tango a proactive and exciting attitude for both the man and the woman.

Dynamics of the Embrace

The primary role of the man in the Argentine tango is to dance around the space of the dance floor while protecting his partner and respecting the space of others and the dance floor itself. The primary role of the woman is to dance surrounding the man, not away or into him. This is a circular dance at the utmost and diagonal at the minimum. It is danced geometrically in three dimensions. It is not a slot dance, nor is it a static dance. The couples travel the floor. The various figures, simple or complex, are used as navigational tools for the man to safely carry his partner in his arms.

In the beginning it is challenging to find the right fit and feel of the embrace. Socially, human beings are conditioned to give others their own space. Here, we willingly go into each other's space. Getting comfortable is a big accomplishment. Even though we embrace in the Argentine tango, there is no reason for anyone to be uneasy within the embrace. It is traditional for the woman to set the limits of her comfort zone. She does so by politely setting her left arm at the distance that works for her. Conversely, she shouldn't approach her partner and throw her body onto him or grip him around the neck. She should prepare for the dance by simply and quietly standing in front of him, allowing him first to encircle her waist at the distance he is proposing. Then she should adjust her left arm while keeping contact, in accordance to her wishes.

The man should not force a woman to dance closer than she wishes. He should suggest the necessary points of contact: the upper arms of the closer side of the embrace touching, with no space between them. A man should not suggest that the woman "give frame," or "give tension," on her right side. The man holds his left arm at the level that he needs her right arm to be.

If a woman is much shorter than a man, he should adjust his encircling right arm a bit higher. If she is taller, his arm should go lower. His hand should try to reach the middle of her back, regardless of his or her height, and rest on part of her right side. At all times and at all heights, the shoulder line of the woman must be horizontal. The man's left hand should be held at the level of her mouth.

The posture of the Argentine tango, with its points of contact, is a natural stance. We are very fortunate to be dancing a root dance that has not been stylized and modified from its original form. The Argentine tango we dance socially today is essentially danced the way it was danced during the golden age of the tango, the late 1930s until the 1950s. Some earlier departures from the root dance formed what we now know as the American and international tango. You can see the influence of the root of the Argentine tango, but the other two have their own posture, mannerisms, and movements, and even different music.

The current trend of the Argentine tango is about 20 years old. Some of the older dancers that were dancing 20 years ago have passed away. Even fewer remain from the days of the 1950s. For the first time in 50 years, a generational difference is occurring. Young dancers are altering the now-classic style of the older generation. As with any popular dance form that has existed for more than 100 years, it remains to be seen which of the old tried-and-true movements will survive alongside today's designer moves created by the younger generation who are self-described transgressors. In any event, this interaction ensures that a next generation will be dancing Argentine tango well into the 21st century, in a modern world craving a good old-fashioned hug.

MYTHS AND MISCONCEPTIONS OF TANGO DANCING

Over the years two of the most frequently asked questions we have heard everywhere we teach are "Why is your instruction different from that of other teachers that I had taken a class with?" and "Why didn't they explain things the way you do?" The answers to both questions are that we can't speak for other teachers and that teachers don't set out to give erroneous, conflicting, or misleading information. Since there is no standard and no school for teachers, the information is often assimilated, understood, and interpreted subjectively.

Many people offering tango lessons get their information by watching other dancers and videos. They may learn by imitating what they think they see. Some may either hold or attend workshops given by traveling teachers, racking up an impressive list of big-name teachers that they have "studied" with. Some may believe that trips to Buenos Aires are enough to use as a credential. Some may be the better and more outgoing dancers in their communities, and they share their styles. Others with a good memory for the figures another dancer has shown may present these figures as a way to learn. Still others may be starstruck, adopting a favorite dancer as a model and proceeding to teach only the star's style of dancing, in exchange for the star's endorsement of their promoter or local teacher. To be fair, most enjoy teaching for the sake of teaching and because the Argentine tango has taken an important place in their lives.

When a person embarks on the journey of learning to dance Argentine tango, he or she will run into as many opinions of teaching as there are individuals teaching tango. The knowledge of tango dancing has been passed on through word of mouth from generation to generation. Because of that, there is no generally accepted syllabus of Argentine tango. How people learn the dance, and subsequently how they teach it, is at best varied and at worst a hodgepodge nightmare for the student. In response, we present some of the most common myths and misconceptions that sooner or later you will be confronted with. This is not meant as a critique, but rather as an observation that will perhaps be helpful to those who are receptive.

Show Me the Basic

The most common misconception is that quickly learning the "basic step" will be enough to help a person avoid wasting time and energy in lessons and enable a dancer to add another rhythm to a collection of steps. To make things worse, a request to show the basics is not usually directed to teachers but to other dancers perceived as having taken the time and effort to attend classes. Many ballroom dances involve a basic step that never deviates, so it is useful to memorize it in order to qualify as a bronze-level beginner. Tango dancing can be learned through a variety of popular patterns that emphasize the principles of direction changes and floor circulation. Given the premise that the social essence of Argentine tango is an improvised traveling dance, a basic step or pattern would be limited in usefulness. It would require that both dancers know the same basic steps, stifling creativity and minimizing variety.

Some of the first tango lessons taught in the United States took place in the parking lots behind a theater following a performance of the critically acclaimed musical revue *Tango Argentino*. Indeed, the first teachers in the 1980s were members of the cast who suddenly found thrilled audience members asking them to teach. When asked to teach, they resorted to the use of choreography they were familiar with on the stage, creating a pattern to satisfy their students who were asking for a basic step. The sequence became known as the *eight-count basic*. It consisted of eight linear steps that started with a back step of the man, included an unusual crossing of the woman's left foot in front of her right foot, and ended with both dancers closing their feet together.

When executed as just another figure inserted in the middle of the dance, the eight-count basic is utilitarian. Because of the repetitive start-and-stop nature of the pattern, it is frustrating and almost worthless, not to mention boring, when used as a way to start to dance on the social floor. Couples can seldom take eight consecutive steps to a prescribed completion on a moderately crowded social dance floor. They will simply be blocked by other couples at any one of the eight stations along the way. The first couples to venture to Buenos Aires in the early 1990s looking for the ultimate in tango dancing found that out very quickly. They learned that the basic step was useless as they bumped their way around seasoned dancers on the dance floor.

Memorizing patterns is contrary to the very essence of the improvised dance. The freedom to move, changing fronts and changing directions while the woman dances around the man and the man dances around the floor, is rooted in solid technique that dancers need in order to create patterns and figures.

When to Cross

Another drawback to the memorization of patterns, in particular the afore-mentioned eight-count basic, is the lack of an obvious or logical reason for the woman to cross her legs. Thus there is the misconception that makes women hesitate and ponder whether, or when, to cross or not to cross the legs. Lacking a clear understanding of the structure of the dance, many jump at the opportunity to become expert dance instructors, offering contradictory answers to a question that is formulated out of ignorance.

We have mentioned the curious and unusual, albeit characteristic, crossing of legs as the couples dance the tango. We have also mentioned that one of the principles of the dance is that the woman dances around the man and the man dances around the floor. This means that the woman never moves into or away from her partner, but around him, in a clockwise or counterclockwise direction. Forced to move to either her right or her left side, the woman has to cross one of her legs to continue progressing in the same direction. If she is surrounding the man to his left side, she will have to cross her left leg behind or in front of her right leg in order to keep her upper body aligned with his upper body. Similarly, if she is going around the man's right side, she will have to cross her right leg behind or in front of her left leg in order to keep her upper body aligned with his upper body.

The answer is actually logical and simple if you remember the code of the tango: The woman crosses her left leg when she needs to move to her right while standing on her right axis. The woman crosses her right leg when she needs to move to her left while standing on her left axis. What creates the need for the woman to move is the action of the man's upper body, which is connected to his right arm embracing her as he navigates around the floor. As she continues to move in one direction, the code is in effect so that the crossing of legs follows the predictable and alternating pattern: One time the cross is behind the support leg, and the next time it is in front of it.

Collect Your Feet

This is a misconception that women in particular take to heart as some way of producing their first attempts at neat footwork. It seems easy enough: Feet together. Pretty, neat feet. However, "feet together" is the wrong thing to be concerned about. Correct foot placement is important. Argentine tango uses the body to displace and transport the legs and feet connected under it. As we walk, there is weight on one leg or the other. As we change axis from one leg to the other, the legs open and close, open and close. The leg with no weight on it is free for the man to place as he changes direction.

A better image is that the upper thighs open and close while passing through the step. If the woman concentrates on "collecting" her feet together, energy is produced in the free foot coming to connect with the other foot of the support leg. This energy in the leg that is supposed to be free, no matter how subtle, creates heaviness and impedes the ability of the man to place the free leg smoothly and freely. It also makes the woman look as heavy as she feels to the man. Men are strong, and they can and will muscle their partners on the dance floor if that is the only way that they can move the women. It's not a comfortable way for either one to dance, nor is it very pleasing to look at. Some women get so carried away with bringing the feet together that they look like soldiers coming to attention at every step.

On Your Toes

Many female dancers seem to dance on their toes. Since most social dancers are not trained ballet dancers, this would be an impossible task for the social dancer. It is true that the weight is placed forward on the metatarsal, the ball of the foot. But that should be the extent of it. (See the distinction in figure 4.4, a and b.) However, when walking backward, she will find it helpful to lead with the base of her curled-up big toe, followed by the metatarsal. She then transfers her body weight over the support leg by elongating the calf to bring her heel down as her partner advances.

Some women seem to like being on their toes all the time, but they should transfer their entire body weight and line to the support leg. At this point the support leg should become elongated so that the nonsupport leg can dangle freely straight down from the hip. Lifting the rib cage to make the body tall on the support leg, which lifts the body enough to make the free leg get shorter, takes care of this. This applies to lateral steps, forward steps, and backward steps. The idea is to always bring your body over the support leg under you. The head, shoulder, breast, and knee are aligned over the support leg.

Try weight changes in place, standing with the feet together, shifting your axis from one leg to the other. This will show you how much the body travels even when standing in place. When dancing with the assistance of another

Figure 4.4 *(a)* Correct: She holds her axis with her heels down. *(b)* Incorrect: She can't hold her axis if she dances on her toes.

person, it is easy to combine a rise on the metatarsal with a lift of the rib cage to produce a clean, confident line completely on the support leg. The free leg dangles prettily from the hip (to be placed in the next direction by the man, producing seamless, weightless, and timely embellishments). If the woman uses her rib cage to lift herself up, she will never hang on the man to achieve her balance or her axis. If both the man and woman make their weight changes correctly and completely, they will be dancing "grounded on the floor." That gives the Argentine tango its specific look and feel.

Cheek to Cheek

It is often observed that couples have their heads together as they dance. It looks so intimate. But if the woman places her head on the man's shoulder or leans her head on his head, her axis line is broken, which makes it difficult for her to achieve and maintain her balance over her support leg. The situation is aggravated if the woman insists on leaving her head glued to her partner's head or shoulder while he tries to produce the subtle but necessary body separations and displacements. It inhibits the man's ability to dance freely and create any kind of figure.

Ladies, be aware of keeping your head up on your vertical axis. If the couple wants the aesthetic look of heads together, it is the man who leans his head toward the woman. He can then move it away when he needs to create space and body displacements. As will be explained in detail in later chapters, bringing the foreheads together in tango serves the purpose of adding another point of contact between the man and the woman. The contact is at the forehead level, not cheek to cheek. Men need to be aware of not pushing with the head connected to the woman's head in order to make space. The shoulders and arms aid in making space as well as in staying on the center axis. Early in the 1930s, the men actually used the head contact as an added element to mark the woman's movements. A better understanding of technique today makes it unnecessary to mark with the head.

The Stranglehold, or the Sticky Woman

Many women will try to imitate a beloved teacher or dancer. If the teacher wraps her arm around the neck of her man in the sexiest embrace, this is all that the student sees (sigh) and in turn tries to imitate. They do not realize that the woman is completely on her own axis and well matched in height to her partner. For the woman, the point of contact of the embrace, regardless of its closeness, is with the inside of her left triceps located directly over his biceps. She places this part of her arm on top of his biceps, with her elbow positioned down. She embraces the man's arm with her arm and always has contact there. If there is any space under the arm, or if her arm does not make contact with his arm, it is very difficult to receive the body mark transmitted through his shoulder and arm. Even in the closest of embraces, this position is still valid. When the woman feels the man creating space by opening his shoulders or sliding his arm away, she should in turn slide her left arm out while maintaining contact. Do not hang on for dear life and impede the effort of the man to mark the step. If he creates space, take it and make use of it. And always remember to keep your weight on the leg closest to the man.

It's Always the Other Leg

When you see a woman or a man doing an embellishment, such as a *boleo* (a leg flick), a *gancho* (a leg hook), a *planeo* (a leg glide), or an *amague* (a feint), the eyes focus on what appears to be the energy of the leg doing the embellishment. But, in fact, the opposite is true. Remember that only one leg, the support leg, has energy in it. The nonsupport leg is always free, dangling. If you produce energy with the free leg to create the embellishment, you will take yourself off your support axis, which will create a position of unbalance. You will also become heavy because you have energy in both legs. You will most likely try to compensate for these two problems by using your partner for support and balance. The unfortunate result will be that you knock yourself and your partner off balance. Another thing to consider is verticality. By remaining true to the technique of being tall on your support leg, you will be vertical on your axis. When doing embellishments, remain vertical on the axis over the support leg. The energy produced is directed upward.

Lead and Follow: A Flawed Partnership

The pure definition of a partnership states that both partners assume 100 percent of the responsibility for the actions of the partnership, and each partner is bound 100 percent to his or her own actions. The Argentine tango is a dance of full partnership, in which both members of the partnership, most commonly referred to as the couple, must contribute 100 percent of their skills, talents, and emotions and assume 100 percent of the responsibilities. By definition, then, the Argentine tango is not a lead-and-follow dance.

If it were merely a matter of semantics or a casualty of translation, the unique concept of la marca, which experienced tango dancers recognize as the profound body language that serves as a communication channel for the couple, could be replaced by ballroom dance's terms of *lead* and *follow*. After all, what counts is the understanding of the concept that governs partner communication in tango dancing and not the desire to classify the dance as the 11th dance of the ballroom circuit.

According to Richard Powers, head of the dance department at Stanford University, Arthur Murray is credited with stating in the 1940s that dance floors were the one place where women preferred to remain submissive. This was a natural consequence of a trend that began in the 1930s when the use of the expression *lead* came to be a synonym for *command*, and *follow* ended up being by default a synonym for *obey*. The emphasis on the pleasure of dancing for each partner had been lost for partners who began calling each other *leads* and *follows*, a subtle yet dehumanizing process of the dance experience.

The 1930s were a time when women's views on suffrage and feminism were a threat to the male-dominated society, so rules requiring women to be gentle and submissive when dancing were ideas welcomed by the rule makers of ballroom dance. The role of the follow was defined as part of a duty for women to let the men lead on the ballroom floor. The role of the lead was then one of a guiding force; the leads were to be the pace makers, the follows their shadows. American views on these matters of dancing roles were mild in comparison to the more chauvinistic attitudes of the British ballroom establishment. Visibly annoyed with women's protests for sexual equality, the male dancers took heart from the fact that, on the dance floor, they were still the masters. It was they who decided when and where any particular step was to be danced. They thought out the patterns of the dance, making it their business to do most of the work while their female partners just made a pretty picture.

The bottom line was that the ladies didn't have much input regarding the male and female roles as a male-controlled dance establishment defined them, except perhaps in the extreme cases where the tightness of an embrace would betray an intention to break their backs. It is against this background of biased hierarchy that newer generations of dancers grew up with a mistaken sense of competition and an adversarial attitude toward each other.

Liberation came in the form of new dances that eliminated contact between dancers. Ironically, the elders of that generation and their descendants were the ones who took to the Argentine tango as an addiction, an obsession, and a way of life. It is for their benefit that the myth of leads and follows needs to be demystified. It is for your benefit that the myth of leads and follows needs to be placed into context, along with the exhilaration contained in the possibilities of full partnership in the tango. Be aware of hypocritical men who like to enunciate in patronizing ways proverbs such as "Men propose, women dispose" to appease what, in their perception, is an unhappy female population. Here is a proverb that can summarize the point we make: "It takes two to tango: one man and one woman."

POSTURE, POSITION, AND MARKING

Among the many traditions that guide the behavior of tango dancers in a public dance hall is the opportunity to engage in conversation during the short interlude between the tangos of a set, commonly known as a *tanda*. When the next tango begins, the sound of the conversations blends with the music for a few seconds. In places where respect for elders is part of the social protocol, dancers wait until the oldest dancer begins to dance.

Gradually the couples embrace, the spoken word dies, and a new dialogue begins. It is an unspoken interchange that goes on between the dancers. And it is based on a language that is unique to the tango dance: *la marcación*, a corporal communication between the dancers that carries the rhythm and melody of the music from the loudspeakers into their bodies and on to the dance floor. This fundamental aspect of tango dancing

tanda—*A set of dance music, usually three or four songs of the same style and often by the same orchestra or another orchestra in the same mode.*

has been systematically ignored, misrepresented, or mistakenly equated to certain aspects of ballroom dances. As a result, many people learn to dance tango without the benefit of understanding the ever-important concept of la marca.

There is not a direct and accurate translation of the Spanish verb *marcar*, as it relates to dancing. The pure definition of *mark* is the action of tagging, branding, or stamping. Those technically challenged define *mark* as the action of leading and following. Both definitions are quite off the mark.

The Spanish language is rich in words that have several meanings. If you add to that the colloquial expressions found in different regions of Spain and in many countries of South America, you may begin to understand why young tango communities sometimes don't have the benefit of understanding the origin of an expression and its application to tango dancing. Argentine people understand the meaning of the word *marca* simply by looking back to early childhood and remembering the young soldiers marching down Avenida de Mayo on Argentina's National Day to the beat and sound of patriotic songs. As soon as they entered school, Argentine children learned to march in and out of class and school. The action of walking to the beat of a drum at a parade or to the stern "left, right" command from a teacher at school is known as *marcar el paso*, to accentuate the way one steps while following a rhythmic pattern.

An experienced female tango dancer expects her partner to mark every motion to her. Many times, if there is no mark, a well-behaved and properly schooled lady will not move. On more than one occasion an experienced female dancer has been heard to say, "You are not marking anything," or "I don't understand or feel your mark." The woman is not asking to be branded with an X on her forehead or to have finger marks on her back at the end of the night. She is requesting la marca. She is requesting that the man contribute his 100 percent to the dance. Since there does not seem to be a fair translation for the words *la marca*, we might as well add this new tango word to our vocabulary and to our tango technique. "So, gentlemen, on your mark, get set, now ready . . . to learn all about la marca."

To understand the concept of la marca, we will review the concepts of good posture and the dynamics of the embrace. In adopting the dancing posture,

Argentine schoolchildren of yesteryear march, "marking the step" into their classroom.

Draftees march, "marking the step" through the streets of Buenos Aires.

the man encircles the woman with his right arm, creating a space where she will dance. The entire left side of her body has contact with the right side of his body. The points of contact are her left upper arm firmly set on his right upper arm, his right upper arm in full contact with her body, and his right forearm and hand gently holding her back (see figure 4.5).

The primary use of la marca is to allow the man to communicate to the woman elements of rhythm and tempo of the music. In return, she will understand when, how, and where to move her legs as her body travels in the embrace.

She Moves, Then He Moves

To be able to dance with the intention of surrounding the man, the woman moves into space created by his marca following the general direction of her shoulder line. In case it is not obvious yet, in Argentine tango, she leads the way and he follows her. She moves, and then he moves. As the man marks the next step, he must wait until she begins the leg extension and advance with his body only when he has felt her metatarsal firmly placed on the floor. At the moment the transfer of weight takes place, her extended leg elongates and her heel touches the floor.

The subtle delay between the motions of the dancers is what creates the sought-after feline elegance of the dancing couple. You can't walk like a cat, because you have only two legs. But an embracing couple, combining both sets of legs, can.

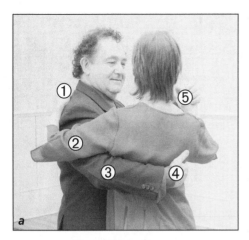
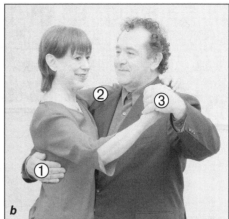

Figure 4.5   Points of contact in the embrace.

Understanding the concept of "he moves me, then he moves" (if you are a woman) or "I move her, then I move" (if you are a man) is a significant step toward developing the natural sway and sensual motion characteristic of the Argentine tango. It takes two to tango, as the cliché says. To sum up, the dissection of a step shows two parts: the contact of the metatarsal with the floor on the upbeat (strong beat) and the elongation of the leg that places the heel in full contact with the floor on the downbeat (weak beat). When each dancer takes the time to travel with confidence in the execution of each step, each contributes to the quality of the dance.

To develop a natural sense for the "she moves, then he moves" concept, visualize the triangle that forms during the transition between steps. As one of the partners reaches full axis, the other has both feet on the ground. The combined position of both dancers' feet forms the vertices of a triangle (figure 4.6). Therefore it is important for both dancers to form a triangle when they step. When walking, the placement of the step should fall near the midpoint between the feet of your partner.

Figure 4.6   With correct placement of the step, the dancers' feet should form a triangle.

MARKING THE THREE STEPS OF THE CODE

For the man to learn this necessary skill, the cooperation of the woman is essential. The woman must concentrate on maintaining a clear and comfortable axis. She should be patient and wait on her axis. Rather than helping by moving on her own, she needs to observe the way her body is being directed by an external force. Her hips must be relaxed so that her upper body is able to disassociate and independently turn on the support leg. As her body is moved from axis to axis, she must remember to have the intention of going around the man when he brings her free leg to the ground.

Marking an Opening

Watch this demonstrated on the DVD

To mark an opening, the man will move the woman in the direction of her free leg.

1. Start with each of you standing on your home axis (right axis for the man, left axis for the woman) with your heels together and your toes pointed outward.
2. Bend your support leg, naturally bringing the woman down so her support leg also bends.
3. Rotate your upper body slightly to your left, opening your left shoulder.
4. Put pressure on her left side with your right arm, causing her right leg to open and reach down to your left.
5. Change your axis to the left leg, and scoop the woman under her shoulder blade with your arm to change her axis to her right leg.
6. Stand up on your left axis, and elongate to allow her upper thighs to join together.
7. Bend your support leg, naturally bringing the woman down so her support leg also bends.
8. Rotate your upper body slightly to your right, opening your right shoulder.
9. Pull her left side with your right arm, causing her left leg to open and reach down to your right.
10. Change your axis to the right leg, and scoop the woman under her shoulder blade with your right arm to change her axis to her left leg.
11. Stand up on your right axis, and elongate to allow her upper thighs to join together.
12. Repeat until la marca for openings is clear, smooth, and easily understood by the woman.

Note: Men can take small side steps while changing axis to increase the amount of control of the woman's opening.

Marking an Inside Cross

To mark an inside cross, the man will move the woman in the direction of her support leg.

Watch this demonstrated on the DVD

1. Stand on your left axis with your heels together and your toes pointed outward.
2. Use your right arm to place the woman on her right axis on your left side.
3. Mark an opening to your right. Her axis changes to her left leg, and your axis changes to your right.
4. Extend your right arm to your right to place her left leg to the right of your right leg.
5. Step back with your left leg, and turn your upper body in the direction of her body.
6. Open your right shoulder and bring the woman's body forward to your right side.
7. Make sure that her right leg crosses inside, between you and her support leg.
8. Bring your right leg to a close without changing weight.
9. Scoop the woman under her shoulder blade with your right arm, and begin turning her to face your left side.
10. Change your axis to your right leg.
11. Turn your upper body to your left, opening your left shoulder.
12. Step back with your left leg in a diagonal, and bring the woman's body forward to your right side.
13. As the woman steps forward, make sure to rotate her upper body gently to face you.
14. Make sure that her left leg crosses inside between you and her support leg.
15. Scoop the woman under her shoulder blade with your right arm, and begin turning her to face your right side. Repeat from step 5 until la marca for inside crosses is clear, smooth, and easily understood by the woman.

Marking an Outside Cross

To mark an outside cross, the man will move the woman in the direction of her support leg.

Watch this demonstrated on the DVD

1. Stand on your right axis with your heels together and your toes pointed outward.

2. Use your right arm to place the woman on her left axis on your right side.

3. Mark an opening to your left. Her axis changes to her right leg, and your axis changes to your left.

4. Hold the woman on her right axis, and change your axis back to your right.

5. Step forward with your left leg into your northwest (forward left diagonal) quadrant.

6. Extend your right lower arm to press against the left side of the woman with your upper arm.

7. Pull gently with your left arm to make the woman step back to your left with her left leg.

8. Make sure that her left leg crosses outside of her support leg.

9. Bring your right leg to a close without changing weight.

10. Scoop the woman under her shoulder blade with your right arm and begin turning her away from you so that her back is toward your right side.

11. Step forward with your right leg into your northeast (forward right diagonal) quadrant.

12. Use your upper body to make the woman step back to your right with her right leg.

13. Make sure that her right leg crosses outside of her support leg.

14. Bring your left leg to a close without changing weight.

15. Scoop the woman under her shoulder blade with your right arm and begin turning her away from you so that her back is toward your left side. Repeat from step 5 until la marca for outside crosses is clear, smooth, and easily understood by the woman.

The way men and women embrace and the posture they assume when dancing tango make it possible for the couple to move their bodies at the same time while their legs follow in synch, out of synch, or not at all. It is the displacement of the bodies that makes the legs move. In the embrace, the man carries the woman as they navigate the dance floor. Men use leverage to propel their bodies and those of their partners; they receive the women's steps with weight changes. Women's legs follow their bodies to provide support, axis, and balance, always carrying the weight on the leg closer to their partners.

To navigate the floor, the man will use diagonal and circular trajectories that revolve around a small number of patterns that are modified to satisfy different situations on the dance floor. We will see that at the core of all patterns, each sequence will be two, three, and four steps long. Each sequence follows the woman's trajectory around the man, using each one of the three stages of the code to make her change direction from right to left and from left to right of the man.

In summary, the woman has now learned how to hold herself on axis, how to allow the free leg to follow her body moving in one of three ways with respect to the support leg and in relation to her partner, and how to transfer her weight to establish a new axis on completion of a step.

The man and woman have also experimented with the techniques of the embrace and the principle of points of contact. This establishes the mechanics by which the man marks the direction, timing, and amplitude of the woman's movements, while the woman manages her axis and allows her body to be carried in the embrace of the man. The man has learned how to make the woman dance around him to avoid colliding with other dancers.

We have now reached the point of introducing the fundamental concepts that define the way the couple moves along the line of dance and around the floor.

Getting Along
in a Circle of Trust

In between turns and gallant compliments let's imagine today living in a foregone time. Don't miss a single beat of this captivating tango, rebellious and overly sweet. Listening to it, how nice it is to dance!

—*Leopoldo Diaz Vélez, "Muchachos comienza la ronda" (1941)*

As we have been stressing, the role of the woman includes elements that contribute to the safe circulation of the couple around the floor. One is the judicious use of the code of the tango; another is the correct way to let her legs follow her body as her body is carried in her partner's embrace. We can't put enough emphasis on the fact that dancing around the man is what produces the look of legs being crossed, as seen from the point of view of the man. In reality, her legs are moving forward or backward on a circular trajectory around the center axis provided by the man. Her upper torso is always turned in the direction of her partner to maintain connection with his upper torso. The effect, from where the man stands, is that in between lateral openings, one of his partner's legs is crossed inside the couple (into him) and the other is crossed outside the couple (away from him). However, the responsibility of circulating around the floor without causing harm is attributed to the man. Polite and civilized behavior on the dance floor is to be expected from everyone who claims to be a good tango dancer. It's not how many steps you can do but how many you can do without infringing on the right of the rest of the dancers to enjoy their time without risking injuries and abuse. The purpose of learning to dance the tango is not to collect steps to impress the foolish but to learn the rules and codes of conduct that are faithfully followed by seasoned dancers around the world.

Occasionally the concept of structure in tango is met with a certain skepticism, if not downright cynicism. Generally the excuses fall under the umbrella of freedom of expression. In some cultures it is fashionable to show aversion to authority figures. Teachers and their concepts of structure may be framed as the works of the tango police. After all, the battle cry is "We are not in Buenos Aires." You will find them everywhere, recklessly using empty geometry, crude acrobatics, and clueless attitudes to endanger those who are trying to mind their own business on the dance floor. Their ignorance of a culture and values that are part of a rich tradition makes them an eyesore on every dance floor they choose as their playground. It is only through education and proper learning that you can avoid becoming a clueless tango dancer and instead set the standard of excellence for others to follow. Tango dancing is a dance of people showing their pride in the way they dance by respecting each other, the music, the dance floor, and the rest of the dancers. The fact that the man is responsible for dancing around the floor makes him more accountable for the behavior of the couple on the dance floor.

THE MAN DANCES AROUND THE FLOOR

As he embraces the woman, the man must be aware that he is first and foremost protecting her by placing his body between her body and the charge of clueless dancers. For most of the dance, as the couple circulates, the man keeps the lady on an outer route with her back always totally to or diagonally to the outside of the floor.

In today's environment, the man should know the fundamental canons of tango dancing:

1. Protect the woman within the embrace.
2. Change her direction around you from one side to the other.
3. Circulate—dance—around the floor by moving the center of the couple.
4. Avoid pushing (leading) your partner and forcing her to walk backward away from you.
5. Avoid pulling your partner and forcing her to walk straight into you.
6. Avoid moving in a straight line in front of each other, which makes it impossible for either one of you to dance around each other.

Imagine a railroad track with the certainty of trains coming from either direction. The most glaring indication that people don't have the proper schooling in tango dancing is that they stand with one foot on each rail, facing an imaginary line of dance. They walk on the track, one leading the other to the light at the end of the tunnel on a collision course with an oncoming train—that is, if they are not run over by another train coming from behind. Some approach the tango as the 11th dance of the ballroom circuit. They teach tango in terms of leading and following. Those who learn how to "lead and follow" see a light at the end of their tunnel vision. They stay on the railroad track, sharing sets of memorized steps until a train runs them over.

Properly educated tango dancers stand on the track in a very different way. The man is on the inner rail, the one closest to the center of the dance floor. The woman is on the outer rail, the one closest to the periphery of the dance floor. At the most basic level, when the man moves to the outer rail, he moves her to the inner rail, effectively trading places and making her dance around him. She will use crosses to change rails and do openings on the same rail. You may ask, "What about the trains?" When the skillful tango dancer, the *bailarin de tango*, sees one coming, he simply steps to the next set of railroad tracks. You may now ask, "Why can't leaders and followers do the same?" Because they don't know that there are multiple tracks instead of one line of dance. You finally ask, "But how does one know that there are other tracks?" Tango dancers are aware of the center of their domain. The man creates a multitude of short tracks that run diagonally left and right from where he is standing at the beginning of every step. This is a fundamental concept of the Argentine tango.

We have important advice for the women who face male partners who don't know the responsibilities of their role. They are easily recognized. They are not aware of the code of the tango. They avoid uttering the word *woman*; instead they use the dehumanizing term *follow*. First, don't assume that you are at fault. Avoid being "led" into backing away or into your partner. Always remember that the structure of the dance requires that you go from one side of your partner to the other. Switch rails to avoid being run over by the proverbial train. That is, move diagonally to your right or left side to go from one of his shoulders to the other one. If he doesn't move, it should be obvious whether you are on his right side or left side. The next move, no matter how or with which leg, has to be toward his other side. When he moves, as is the most common occurrence of the dance, you may find yourself on the same side of the man at the end of a step. Even though you went for the other side, his axis moved and so did the center of your trajectory and the relative position of his shoulders. That is why it is important to understand body positions and recognize them as you dance.

BODY POSITIONS

Seasoned tango dancers are constantly aware of where they are with respect to each other. They know which axis they are on. They know which of the three steps of the code is being initiated. That is because the man marks each one of her moves and the woman understands the mark and responds. The talent of being able to dance on the spur of the moment, the fundamental component of improvisation, is complemented by a clear knowledge and recognition of body positions. After you and your partner read the material individually or together, practice together, concentrating on your respective roles. Avoid telling one another what to do, and be honest with yourself.

Home Position

Watch this demonstrated on the DVD

This is the initial body alignment assumed at the start of the dance. It is also the ending position of many patterns. Understand and recognize this position, because you will be at it many times throughout a dance. In many cases it acts as a period at the end of a sentence. Begin by standing while facing each other and assuming the embrace position. If a partner is not available at this time, use your imagination and concentrate on your gender-specific role. The man establishes his axis on his right leg and invites the woman to change her weight and set her axis on her left leg by pulling her gently with his right arm against the right side of his body. The woman should feel a gentle pull on her back, inviting her to set her axis on her left leg. She brings the left side of her body into the right side of his body. To keep a clear point of contact, her left arm should rest on the man's right arm. There shouldn't be any space between their arms. We call this position *home*, *neutral*, or *position 1* (see figure 5.1). From now on each one of you should own (know) your home (position).

The woman needs to be aware that home is on the right side of the man's body. We refer to each side of the man's body as one shoulder or the other. She should expect to leave home going into the direction of the man's left shoulder. She should also be aware that to move to the other shoulder from home, she would use her free leg (her right). The step will be an opening as her right leg separates from the left leg, reaching in the direction of the man's left shoulder. The woman will move when she is gently but firmly brought down from her left axis. The man indicates his partner's movement with a slight left rotation of his upper body. His right arm applies pressure on the woman's left side to bring her to another axis.

Figure 5.1 Home position, with the man on his right axis and the woman on her left axis.

Salida Position

This position is found after the dancers move laterally toward the left side of the man from the home position (see figure 5.2a). The name is derived from the Spanish expression *salir a bailar*, which translates as "exiting to dance." Typically this position is assumed after the first step taken from the home position. This is how it is done:

Watch this demonstrated on the DVD

1. Assume the home position.
2. The man marks an opening to his left.
3. The woman reaches with her right leg toward the man's left shoulder.
4. The man transfers the woman's weight to her right axis.
5. The woman bends her right leg and drops her right heel to claim the new axis.
6. The man transfers his weight to his left leg and elongates his upper body.
7. The woman elongates with the man's embrace and presents her right axis to the man.

The man may switch axis in place at the salida position. In that case, the dancers are said to be in the cross-feet system as opposed to parallel system. Simply, their axes are on the same leg—in this case, the right leg for both.

Outside Right Position

This position occurs when either dancer advances with the right leg on the right side of the other. For example, from the salida position the man walks forward with his right leg on the right side of the woman and

Watch this demonstrated on the DVD

marks a back step for her, which she executes with her left leg (see figure 5.2b). He turns his upper body to his right to face his partner, executing what we have called an inside cross, since his right leg seems to be crossed

Figure 5.2 Moving from *(a)* salida position to *(b)* outside right position.

inside the couple from the woman's perspective. From the home position, if the man steps back with his left leg and marks an inside cross to his right, the woman will step forward with her right leg, keeping her body turned in to him. She will execute an inside cross of her right leg.

Outside Left Position

Watch this demonstrated on the DVD

This position is the mirror image of the outside right position as the dancers are to the left of each other. In this case, the inside cross is done with the left leg of the person moving forward. Although it is very unusual to get into the outside left position from the salida position in a real dancing situation, let's get you in the salida position but with the woman on the left side of the man. The man accomplishes that by a combination of actions that modify the mark to get into the salida position from the home position. Mainly, he needs to extend his embrace more to his left while stepping short with his left leg. With the woman slightly to his left in the salida position, the following occurs:

1. The man turns to his left, opening his left shoulder.
2. The man steps back with his right leg, keeping most of his weight on his left leg to avoid transferring his weight.
3. The man guides the woman, pulling her into his left side.
4. The woman bends her right leg, staying on axis while reaching down and forward with her left leg.
5. The man transfers his weight completely to his right axis, keeping both bodies turned in to each other.
6. The woman completes her inside cross with her left leg, transferring her weight to her forward leg.

It is also unusual for the man to advance on an outside left position in the parallel system. More likely, the man will change weight in place at the salida position and walk on her left side with his left leg in the cross-feet system. At this point, it is important to understand the concept of body positions and begin to recognize them as you dance.

NO MATTER WHERE YOU GO, THERE YOU ARE

A useful concept for orderly circulation around the dance floor is to imagine the couple traveling around the floor using segments of circular trajectories that are either clockwise or counterclockwise. In other words, when the man embarks on a series of movements turning to his left, the couple will advance, turning counterclockwise in the same general direction as the imaginary line of dance.

If the man begins a series of movements turning to his right, the couple will advance, turning clockwise in the same general direction as the imaginary line of dance. A commonsense guideline for the man, then, is to combine elements of left and right trajectories that look more like seesaws or wedges connected with each other follow the imaginary line of dance. Many well-known patterns achieve the purposes mentioned previously. Their simplicity and logic are such that many people have learned how to do them without knowing why they do them. You have the advantage of learning not only how to do patterns but also why, when, and for what purpose. You are on your way to acquiring a mastery of floor craft.

La Base

In chapter 3 you learned a six-step pattern called la base [la BAH-say]. It is one of the various blueprints that we use as a starting point in the process of learning. The meaning of the word *base* in Spanish is very clear for teachers from Argentina. It means foundation, platform, and support. Unfortunately, when translated to English, it has been notoriously mistaken as "the basics." We favor its use as an intuitive, simple, and logical sequence of body positions that a dancer can use to recognize where any sequence begins and ends. Tango is multifaceted. The same sequences may be looked at from different angles as the dancers find their preferences to explore the infinite possibilities of genuine improvisation.

The power of la base resides in the fact that it uses the six unique root movements that are possible with the use of two legs: one opening with each leg, one forward step with each leg, and one back step with each leg. You will hear these movements defined as one side step with each leg, one forward step with each leg, and one back step with each leg. The important thing to remember is to execute all steps with the intention of getting around a partner and not, we repeat, *not* to walk into or away from a partner as if standing in front of each other on a railroad track with one foot on each rail.

The key to understanding the real meaning of tango improvisation is knowing beforehand that when everything is said and done, there are only three unique steps for each leg, for a grand total of six steps to dance the tango. Our goal is to teach you how to think in terms of using these six root moves to explore the infinite possibilities of the tango. When a man and a woman face each other and execute la base, they mirror each other's steps. That alone is why la base is one of the most powerful patterns used to get on the dance floor right away.

Let's get ready to practice la base starting from the home position. As always, should a partner be unavailable at this time, use your imagination and follow the instructions for your specific role. See figure 5.3 for a diagram of the six stages of la base.

Watch this demonstrated on the DVD

Base 1. Base 1 begins at home position. The man marks the woman an opening to his left. He opens "long" laterally with his left to receive her side step. The woman responds to the mark by opening "short" laterally with her right leg reaching toward the man's left shoulder. The lateral move ends at the salida position.

Base 2. Base 2 begins at salida position. The man marks the woman an outside cross to his left. He moves forward around the woman's right side. He forms a triangle with his right foot, placing it halfway between her feet, in a line in front of the tip of his left foot. The woman responds to the mark by coming down from her right axis, extending her left leg back, and keeping her weight on the front leg, naturally bent to stay connected to her partner. The move ends at the outside right position.

Base 3. Base 3 begins at the outside right position. The man marks the woman a back opening diagonally to his left. He advances, placing his left foot in a line in front of the tip of his right foot and the tip of her right foot. The woman responds to the mark by opening her right leg back in a diagonal toward her own right side with the intention of intercepting the trajectory of the man. The move ends at the salida position.

Base 4. It begins at salida position. The man advances, opening forward with his right leg on a diagonal to his right, while at the same time turning to his left. He forms a triangle with his right foot placed halfway between the woman's feet. The woman responds to this mark by turning to her left and opening with her left leg in the direction of the man's right shoulder. As he transfers his weight to his right axis, he places the lady on her left axis. It ends at the home position.

Base 5. It begins at home position. The man marks the woman an inside cross to his right. He steps back, placing his left leg in line with the heel of his right foot. Keeping his weight on the right leg, he brings her forward. The woman responds to the mark with an inside cross with her right leg advancing around the man's right side. She forms a triangle with her right foot placing it halfway between his feet, in a line in front of the tip of her left foot. It ends at outside right position.

Base 6. It begins at the outside right position. The man marks the woman a forward opening. He steps back, placing his right leg back in a diagonal with the intention of intersecting the trajectory of the woman. The woman responds to the mark by placing her left foot in a line in front of the tip of her right foot and the tip of his right foot. As he transfers his weight back to his right leg, he places the lady on her left axis. La base ends at the home position.

You have successfully used the three unique steps with each leg and the three body positions you know so far to dance your first pattern. After you feel comfortable with the simplicity and ease of execution of la base, play a tango and begin adjusting the timing of your body positions to the beat of the tango.

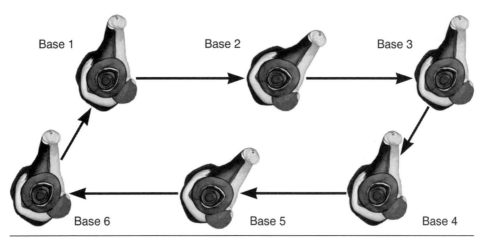

Figure 5.3 The six stages of la base.

Consider la base as a round trip consisting of two one-way routes. Base 1-2-3 is what we call the "front end" of la base. Base 4-5-6 is what we call the "back end" of la base. If you consider la base from another reference point, after you do base 1 and base 2, you will notice that base 3-4-5 is a forward change of front to the left for the man (forward-open-back). It is also a backward change of front to the left for the woman (back-open-forward). Likewise, base 6-1-2 is a backward change of front to the left for the man (back-open-forward). It is also a forward change of front to the left for the woman (forward-open-back). Base 1 and base 4 are powerful steering opportunities for the man since he can open by turning to his left as much as he wants or not at all. Finally, in terms of the mechanics of leg motion, base 2, base 3, and base 4 are forward leg motions for the man and backward leg motions for the woman. Base 5, base 6, and base 1 are backward leg motions for the man and forward leg motions for the woman. At this point, you are ready to understand that there are no side steps in tango. The illusion of side steps is a consequence of dancing right or left of each other. The third forward motion, done with the right leg, resolves into a lateral opening as the dancer turns to his or her left. Likewise, the third backward motion, done with the left leg, resolves into a lateral opening as the dancer turns to his or her left. This is because of the circular trajectory that results from the intention of always trying to dance around each other.

Simple Salida

The dictionary translation of *salida* is "exit"; however, don't be misled by an exit sign thinking that it indicates the entrance to a tango dance hall. There are many nuances used in the Spanish language to describe tango jargon. The word derives from the verb *salir*; used in the context of tango, it actually means "enter," as in entering the dance floor. Indeed la salida is universally recognized as being the one pattern everyone knows, whether as part of *cruzada—From cruzar. The action of crossing the legs.*

some memorized routine or within the context of the structure of the tango as you are about to learn it. It is a four-count sequence on a diagonal trajectory to the man's left quadrant, making it likely to be used as the initial pattern. Upon completion, the dancers assume a new body position called *cruzada*. This position is identical to the home position for the man as he stands on his right axis. Although the woman stands on her left axis as in the home position, her left foot is crossed in front of her right foot. Instead of finishing with the inside heels touching, the external part of the feet are touching. The cruzada position is a major link to the beginning and end of many patterns.

La salida complies with the code of the tango and satisfies the principle of the woman dancing around the man and the man dancing around the woman. At every position of the four stages of la salida, the man marks the woman a step to his left side. As soon as the woman begins her motion, with the intention to dance around the man, he moves in the same direction, effectively keeping her on his right side at the end of the step. It is only at the third stage that the man stops, creating space for the woman to move to his left side on the next step. As he brings his feet together with a weight change, her left foot travels in a diagonal to her right side. This produces the crossing of her feet that characterizes the cruzada position.

La salida starts from the home position. The dancers face each other, with the man on his right axis and the woman on her left axis. You must totally understand la base in order to continue.

Watch this demonstrated on the DVD

Salida 1. The first step of la salida is identical to base 1, the first step of la base. It begins at the home position and ends at the salida position.

Salida 2. The second step of la salida is identical to base 2, the second step of la base. It begins at the salida position and ends at the outside right position.

Salida 3. The change from continuing la base begins at the outside right position. The man marks the woman a back opening diagonally to his left as in base 3. He advances with a forward opening, diagonally aiming his left foot to his left forward quadrant. The woman responds to the mark by opening her right leg back in a diagonal with the intention of intersecting the trajectory of the man. As the man transfers his weight to his left leg, his body stops moving forward. He brings the woman to the salida position using a diagonal trajectory to his left side. The woman bends her right leg, transfers her weight to it, and begins elongating. Because the man matched the lady's back opening to his left by continuing moving to his left with a forward opening, he is still blocking her from going to his left side. She remains on his right side.

Salida 4. Without any further forward motion, the man brings his right foot next to his left foot and transfers his weight, turning his upper body slightly to his left. The woman responds to his mark by allowing the man to bring her up on her right axis and rotating her right hip gently to her left. This causes her upper thighs to cross, clearing a path for her left shoe to back straight into the outside or right side of her right shoe. The man exerts pressure with his right arm to bring her to his left side. She responds by allowing her left leg to travel straight back in a diagonal to his left side, crossing in front of her right leg, bending both knees, one behind the other. The position is technically identical to the home position because their hips are facing each other. The man is on his right axis; the woman is on her left axis with her thighs closed. Visually the only difference is that her left shoe is on the outside rather than on the inside of her right shoe.

Let's analyze la salida from the man's position with respect to the woman's leg movements. Salida 1 is an opening with her right leg. Salida 2 is an outside cross with her left leg. Salida 3 is an opening with her right leg. Salida 4 is an inside cross with her left leg. She has moved in accordance with the code of the tango even when her intention to dance around the man was blocked by the man moving to his left on every step except the fourth. As you learned earlier, tango dancers don't mirror each other's trajectories. La salida is a typical example (see figure 5.4). If you envision a triangle, the man moves on the two sides, and the woman travels on the hypotenuse.

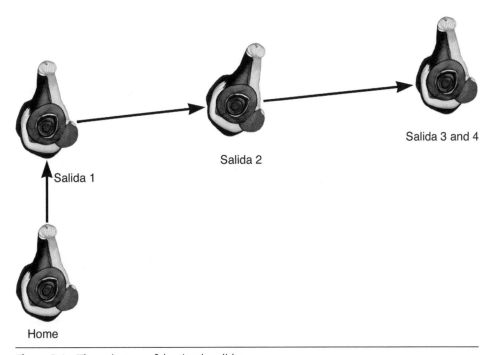

Salida 3 and 4

Salida 2

Salida 1

Home

Figure 5.4   The trajectory of the simple salida.

Resolution

Watch this demonstrated on the DVD

The resolution is a four-count pattern that may be initiated from the home, outside right, or cruzada positions. It includes a change of direction from left to right and ends at the home position. Review la base and identify base 3 and base 4 as the first two steps of the resolution. Review la salida and understand that base 3 and base 4 (or the resolution) can be initiated from salida 4, the cruzada position. These are examples of the thinking process involved in improvising from a solid technical base and a sound understanding of the structure of the dance.

Since the resolution will likely be started right after a salida, assume the cruzada position. Remember also that at the end of la salida, the woman has been moving on a diagonal to her right quadrant, intersecting the trajectory of the man at salida 4.

Resolution 1. This is almost identical to base 3 except that the woman is standing with her legs crossed; she has her axis on the left foot. The man exerts pressure with his right arm into the left side of her body to mark the woman a back opening to his left along the same diagonal she was moving on during the salida. She responds to the mark by resuming the second back step with the right leg, which is always a diagonal. At the same time, the man advances straight forward with his left leg. He places his left foot in line in front of the tip of his right foot and right behind the heel of her left foot, forming a triangle with his left foot and her two feet. As the man transfers his weight forward to his left axis and closes with his right leg, he uses his right arm to bring the woman up on her right axis, assuming the salida position. The compound effect of the man advancing forward and the woman moving across him in a diagonal to his left creates the illusion that the man has turned to his right and is now on her left side. He is on her left side, but he accomplished that by moving her to his left.

Resolution 2. This is very much the same as base 4. The man continues his forward motion while turning to his left to convert the forward opening of his right leg into a lateral opening to his right side. The woman, with her axis firmly on her right leg, responds to the mark by allowing her upper body to go with the embrace of the man. She lets her left leg open "long" in the direction her body is being taken—that is, to the man's right shoulder. The man keeps his right arm tucked to his side and matches her "long" left step, altering the rule of opening "short" to the right. As he transfers his weight to his right leg, his body stops moving. Without any further motion to his right side, the man closes his upper thighs and elongates, allowing his trailing leg to come together with the right leg, but weightless. He scoops the woman under her shoulder blade with his right arm, bringing her to his right side. They end at the home position.

Resolution 3. From the end of resolution 2 at the home position, the man marks the woman a change of axis in place, releasing the pressure of his right hand on the right side of her back. The woman responds to the mark by dropping her right foot to the floor without opening her thighs and changing axis in place. He also changes axis in place, converting their position to a salida position. Experienced dancers who dance with the music will match resolution 3 with the last beat of the tango they are dancing. That is why resolution 3 is sometimes called a tango close, in reference to the way the feet are closed in this position.

Resolution 4. If the music continues, the man opens his right leg diagonally back into his right quadrant to intersect the forward step of the woman. He changes axis to return to the home position in preparation for the beginning of another salida and to match the four-beat tempo of the music. He marks the woman a forward step into him. She responds by opening forward with her left leg with her shoe pointing toward the right shoulder of the man. The resolution ends at the home position.

To advance gradually in a counterclockwise direction around the dance floor, veering in and out to avoid falling into the center of the floor, the man must keep in mind three very important concepts. First, make the woman dance around him; second, change the direction in which she dances around him; and third, alternate the use of trajectories into his left and right quadrant. The resolution consists of one step into the man's left quadrant and three steps into his right quadrant. You should be aware that the resolution can be overused and sometimes abused, when "lead and follow" dancers tuck it right after la salida as part of a memorized eight-count basic pattern. Its main purpose is to reach the end of the dance with a tango close, or to complete a sequence. Although it is the most basic way to continue after the completion of a salida (see figure 5.5), parts of or a complete resolution are used during sequences where the dancers trade places around each other.

When a salida is combined with a resolution, you can properly phrase the eight beats of the tango. Every four steps there is a pause (salida 4 and resolution 4). Be aware of men who use resolution 4 to start to dance. They use the last step of the resolution as the first step of a memorized count of eight that does not keep time with the music. That is not a problem unless you hear things such as "Do this on five" or other equally mystifying instructions such as "One, two, three, four . . ." to have learners back blindly into the line of dance on their very first step. Drilling men and women to memorize patterns so the man can "lead" them and the women can "follow" them produces dancers who are likely to become a liability on a crowded dance floor. The eight-count basic is obsolete for learning to dance the Argentine tango.

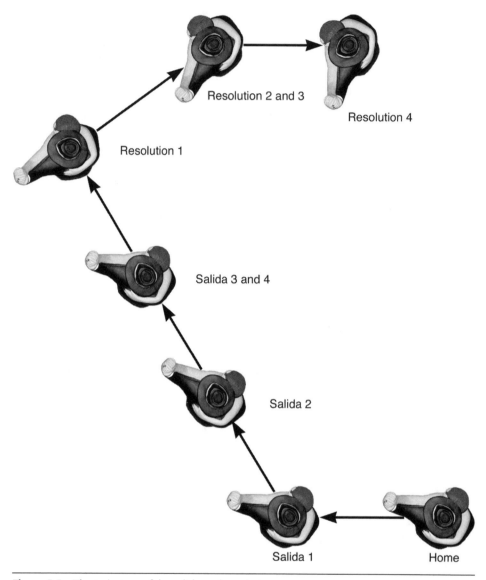

Resolution 2 and 3

Resolution 4

Resolution 1

Salida 3 and 4

Salida 2

Salida 1

Home

Figure 5.5   The trajectory of the salida and resolution.

Cambio de Frente

Watch this demonstrated on the DVD

Unbeknownst to the man (until now) is that his resolution 1 and resolution 2 steps (base 3 and base 4 if you are a quick learner) are also two steps of the code of the tango. Primarily the woman executes the code as she dances with the intention of going around the man. But it is the man's responsibility to mark every step of the code in order to place the woman's body exactly where his intended pattern requires it. So it makes sense for the man to learn what he is doing. Let's analyze resolution 1 and resolution 2 in terms of the root steps covered in chapter 3.

Resolution 1 is an inside cross to the left as far the other dancer is concerned. As the man's left leg moves forward, his upper body turns to acknowledge the presence of the woman on his left. From her perspective, the man's left leg is crossed in front of his right leg, inside their bodies. Although we are addressing the man's use of the steps of the code as part of the resolution and *cambio de frente* (change of front), the learning process is applicable to both genders because in chapter 6 the *woman* will be called to use the code in cambios de frente for *giros* (turns). Resolution 2 is a forward step of the outside leg, which converts into a lateral opening as the man turns to his left, with the intention to dance around the woman's right axis.

A change of front occurs when resolution 3 is replaced with an outside back cross, completing the third step of the code. As a result, from the woman's vantage point, the man's left leg appears crossed behind his right leg, outside the space shared by both dancers.

Assume the cruzada position since a cambio de frente is a second option often used right after a salida. Remember that at the end of the salida, the woman has been moving on a diagonal, intersecting the trajectory of the man at salida 4.

Step 1. Technically this step is resolution 1, which is the same as base 3. The man starts from his right axis while the woman is on her left axis, both assuming the cruzada position. The strategy used by the man is to hold the woman in place as he walks around, changing his front around her. Therefore he must mark the step to the woman so she moves laterally to his left without backing off in order to open a clear path for him to move forward.

Step 2. Technically this step is resolution 2, which is the same as base 4. The man keeps his right arm straight and tucked in to mark an opening to the woman's left in place. She responds by letting her body rotate on her right axis and her leg open "long" in the direction her body is turned by the man. While turning to his left, the man opens forward "short" with his right leg. The effect is a lateral opening in the forward direction. When the man changes his weight to his right leg, the woman responds by changing her weight to her left axis.

Step 3. To complete the change of front (cambio de frente), the man will continue advancing in the same direction, stepping back with his left leg. At the same time, he marks the woman an inside cross to his right side, assuming the outside right position. She responds to the mark with a forward step with her right leg, her right foot turned to point to the man and her upper body turned to face the man. From the man's perspective, her right leg is crossed inside in front of her left leg. From her perspective, his left leg is crossed outside behind his right leg. To reinforce the equal partnership afforded by the tango, we'd like to point out to the woman that the positions of their bodies at this point are identical to base 2 except that the woman is going forward and the man is backing up. This should also encourage dancers to hone their technique regardless of gender.

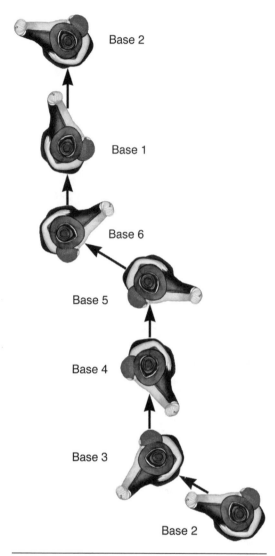

Base 2

Base 1

Base 6

Base 5

Base 4

Base 3

Base 2

Figure 5.6 The trajectory of consecutive changes of front to the left.

The cambio de frente is not a pattern with an end but a link into another pattern. From this position, the man has several options in how to continue:

1. Mark the woman an identical cambio de frente (see figure 5.6), ending at base 2 at the outside right position. In other words, complementary cambios de frente return to the same position where they started. La base, la salida, and the resolution are logical ways to continue from this point. Put the book down and try them all. Visualize and improvise.

2. Bring your right foot together with your left while keeping your axis on your left leg. Mark the woman an inside cross to your left by turning her upper body to point to your left shoulder. The woman should respond to this new mark simply by letting her upper body turn on her right axis and stepping forward with her left leg and reaching for the man's left shoulder. As soon as her left foot lands on the floor, change your weight to your right axis and turn her upper body on her left axis to assume the cruzada position. The woman should respond to the mark by letting her upper body be turned on her left axis into the man. She should assume the cruzada position by crossing her free leg through the back door. Since she is already standing on her left leg, she needs to cross her right leg behind the left leg, keeping the toes pointing outward so the feet form an inverted V. Of course, it is important for the woman to remember to end with her knees bent and her heels down. A logical continuation from here would be another cambio de frente, a resolution, or even resumption of la base.

3. If the last step (outside cross) of the cambio de frente is taken across the grain of the line of dance, once the man changes his weight to his left leg,

he may mark a second forward step for the woman. The woman responds to the mark by advancing with her outside (left) leg. The man intersects her trajectory by stepping back with his right leg into a diagonal to receive the forward step of the woman. This is the home position. A sequence has ended. In preparing for a new start, the man must be aware of the need to direct his left opening into the direction of the line of dance, using a back diagonal into his back left quadrant.

Although it is the man who sees a couple in front of him backing up and has the responsibility of taking action to avoid a collision, it is also the man who backs up against the flow and gets blamed for using poor judgment. It is rarely the case for men who know better to purposely decide to become a liability on the dance floor. In the majority of cases, men who try to lead, women who insist on following, and other technically challenged dancers cause problems for other dancers on the floor. They try to follow a script regardless of where their leading and following take them.

It is never a good idea to back straight into the flow of the dance because it could create a problem for couples following too closely from behind who are thus unable to avoid running into you. A tango dancer knows never to charge (lead) into his partner or pull (follow) away from her partner. Rather, as he makes the woman dance in circular trajectories around him, the man circulates, making judicious use of the openings to steer the couple in diagonals left or right to change fronts. The amount of turning can be anywhere from a slight veering to a complete 180-degree turn, placing the man in a position to move backward while advancing into the line of dance. These concepts can't be repeated often enough.

A combination of a salida, double cambio de frente ending on a second salida, or la base covers a significant amount of space in a relatively linear trajectory without falling into the center of the dance floor. To be honest, being able to complete it with other dancers around is quite a feat. The trajectory of la salida has a gentle bias to the forward left quadrant of the man. That's why it is important for the man to face the outside of the dance floor with the line of dance on his forward left quadrant. The trajectory continues with a double left-side loop (first with the man walking around the woman in a counterclockwise fashion to the outer tracks of the line of dance), followed by a mirror walk of the woman around the man that continues the tendency to drift out to the edge of the dance floor, and ending with another gentle bend to the left that brings the couple to the inner tracks of the line of dance. The level of difficulty decreases as the man develops his ability to mark and carry the woman in his embrace. He becomes a better navigator using each segment of the pattern to make adjustments to sort out obstacles on the dance floor. He also learns to bend the trajectories to make each segment more circular, thus requiring less linear space.

Another popular version of la salida is performed in the cross-feet system. We have mentioned that when dancers face each other, they move by using opposite legs (that is, one dancer moves the right leg while the other dancer uses the left leg), in what is called the parallel system. In tango dancing, it is possible for each person to move while using the same leg (that is, both dancers move the right leg at the same time), in what is called the cross-feet system. To change from parallel to cross-feet system, one of the dancers can either hold a step or double-step. This is done primarily by the man as part of his strategy to decide on a given trajectory or to add flair to the footwork. It can also occur as a result of miscommunication between the man and the woman. This happens in the early stages of learning when the fourth step of la base (base 4) is answered with the third step of the resolution (resolution 3). The weight change in place at resolution 3 puts the dancers in the cross-feet system. If at least one of the dancers realizes what happened, then they can make the necessary adjustment. Keep in mind that there are no mistakes in the tango if you concentrate on dancing and not on which step comes next.

La Salida Cruzada

You should be familiar and comfortable with the structure of la base in order to properly learn and understand the structure of la salida cruzada. Its trajectory is shown in figure 5.7.

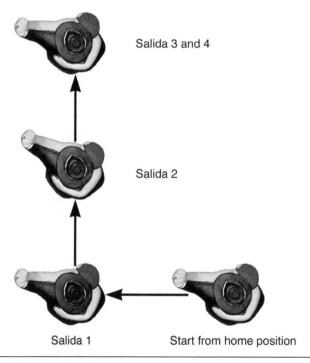

Salida 3 and 4

Salida 2

Salida 1   Start from home position

Figure 5.7   The trajectory of la salida cruzada.

Step 1. Assume the home position. The first step is a lateral, or side step, to the man's left quadrant, except that the man opens "short," altering the rule of opening "long" to the left. To switch to the cross-feet system, the man holds the woman on her right axis and changes weight to his right axis in place.

> Watch this demonstrated on the DVD

Step 2. The second step for the woman is identical to her base 2. The man marks an outside cross of her left leg into his left quadrant. The woman responds to the mark by stepping back with her left leg in the direction of the man's left quadrant. At the same time, the man advances by using his left leg, which is outside the shared space of the couple. He has the option to place his left leg anywhere in his left quadrant, always forming a triangle with his left foot and the woman's two feet. The body position is a modified outside right because the man's step is a forward opening rather than an inside cross.

Step 3. The man shifts his weight completely to his left leg and pushes with the right side of his upper body to mark the woman a back diagonal opening with her right leg. She responds to the mark by anchoring her left foot firmly on the ground and allowing her right leg to be lifted and sent back by the man's forward motion. The man steps forward with his right leg into the space being cleared by the woman's right leg.

Step 4. Without breaking his forward motion, the man leaves his left leg extended behind and bends his right leg to put weight on it. He marks the woman a diagonal to his left with a rotation of his upper body, bringing himself up on axis by straightening his right knee, ready to go with his left leg. The woman responds to the mark by anchoring her right leg firmly on the ground and letting her left leg cross in front of her right leg, following a back diagonal toward the left quadrant of the man. The man holds a step with his left leg, returning them to the parallel system; therefore, he has the same options to continue from the cruzada position.

In this chapter you have learned several important concepts about dancing as a couple. The woman should remember to move with the intention of dancing around the man's right or left side. The man should continue to focus on navigating the dance floor. He should feel comfortable using lateral openings to steer the couple, crisscrossing the imaginary line of dance. Both the man and woman must be aware of the body positions already learned. You should recognize them and concentrate on perfecting each one of them.

Most important of all is to understand the importance of *not* using the concepts of leading and following that are typical of all other dances. Dances that require leading and following neither require the man to embrace the lady nor require the lady to dance around the man. If you still are thinking in terms of leading and following, please review chapters 3, 4, and 5 before proceeding. To advance to the next level, you need to understand that the woman moves in the man's embrace *now*, not after taking time to figure out the "lead," process the proper "follow," and then order the brain to move the body. By then the music is several beats ahead of the movement. Show us lead-and-follow tango dancing, and we'll show you a couple that is not dancing to the music.

In chapter 6 you will discover the structure of the tango and learn the inner workings of turns, or *giros*. New body positions will be introduced so that you can learn how to do displacements while turning around each other. But first, put the book down, play some music, and embrace your partner. Relax and let the body dance. Dance naturally with solid, clear, and consistent weight changes. As you strive not to be a stiff tango dancer, allow the upper body to disassociate from the lower body. Let the body move the hips and let the hips carry the legs. Don't miss a single beat as you listen to the music and begin to realize how nice it is to dance tango.

6

What Goes Around Comes Around

To dance a tango, begin from a common choreographic theme and make use of the movements in vogue at the time in which you begin to dance it. Then, incorporate your personal expression, and let it become your distinctive tango dancer lineage.

—*Carlos Estevez "Petroleo," 1940s tango innovator*

Although people have been dancing tango since the last decades of the 19th century, there is no solid evidence of how the dance looked until the first decade of the 20th century. The way people were dancing in Buenos Aires around 1900 somehow made its way to Europe, and something about the dance appealed to the hedonistic Parisian society. Drawings, posters, and photos from that era don't tell how it was actually danced. During those first two decades of the 20th century, a mythical style of dancing called *canyengue* is supposed to have appeared, taken the dance halls by storm, and then mysteriously disappeared without leaving a trace of how it looked. Not even the tango-crazy Parisians ever made mention of the word *canyengue*.

The word *canyengue* has two accepted definitions. One describes a streetwise and deliberate way of walking, with a lazy, and at the same time taunting, attitude attributed to some elements of society employed at the docks and slaughterhouses. The other one defines a rhythmic effect first attributed to a bass player named Leopoldo Thompson (1890-1925) that consists of hitting the instrument with both the free hand and the arc of the bow. Interestingly enough, there are plenty of recordings ranging from the time of the Francisco Canaro orchestras up to the compositions of Astor Piazzolla where the *efecto canyengue* (canyengue effect) can be clearly heard and recognized. Yet there is not a speck of evidence about an alleged dancing style called canyengue. We believe that folklore led to misunderstandings between those who told tales about loving to dance to the canyengue rhythms favored by many orchestras and those who confused it with the existence of a peculiar dancing style.

Further into the first quarter of the 20th century, tango in Buenos Aires seems to have been danced along social lines. The upper class embraced a sanitized version of the repatriated tango from Paris and made it their dance of choice at the Parisian-style cabarets. The disenfranchised class continued to cross-pollinate the tango with cultural nuances and traditions from every corner of the world that were represented in the city's melting pot. Sex, drugs, and tango happened way before rock 'n' roll. Unfortunately there is very little evidence that can serve as a good point of departure for studying the evolution of the dance. Of course there are lots of mythological dancers, such as Casimiro Ain, who is purported to have danced for the pope, saving the tango from excommunication and eternal condemnation. Then there is Ovidio Bianquet, aka Cachafaz, who has been surrounded by an aura of supernatural dimensions. The only existing 30-second clip available from *El Tango*, the first film shot in Argentina, shows Cachafaz carrying longtime partner Carmencita Calderon in his armpit and frantically stepping around her. This uninspiring scene can only be associated with tango because of the sound track and, of course, the name of the film.

Somehow, a major transformation in the way tango was danced seems to have taken place in the late 1930s, although it is not clear what it was that was being transformed. We know that the music itself had undergone major changes since the 1920s. The generation that came of age toward the end of the 1930s had grown up in the wake of the Great Depression and witnessed the grief that the untimely death of singer Carlos Gardel had produced in their elders. Tango dancing had fallen out of favor and was declared dead in a historic newspaper headline.

From the many unheralded dancers of the time, Carlos Alberto Estevez, aka Petroleo, has emerged as one of the leading innovators who introduced the concepts of *giros* (turns), *enrosques* (corkscrews), and *sacadas* (displacements). His nickname means oil, as in crude oil, because of the dark color of the wine he liked to drink. Estevez is credited as being one of the leading minds behind a new approach to tango dancing based on circular trajectories, which, structurally, form the foundation on which contemporary dancing is based.

sacada—*A displacement.*

The emerging set of techniques was based on figures in which the woman moves around the man and the man trades places with the woman, using changes of front, displacements, and a new set of body positions. Dancers from all over the city began to recognize that change was inevitable. Gradually they began to incorporate their own spice into the new luscious recipe. However, since one of the codes of conduct of the greatest tango dancers of Argentina is to shun imitation, it is important to take notice and underline the special talent and uncanny ability that are required to do things that others do, but better and differently. Since the 1940s, those codes of ethics have led to the development of recognizable styles of dancing characteristic of various neighborhoods. Although to the untrained eye those styles may appear different on the surface, they are rooted in the same principles developed and perfected by people known mostly by their first names or nicknames like Petroleo, El Negro Lavandina, Tarila, Kalisei, Toto, and Mingo. What is significant about all these and other innovators is that they realized the importance of the woman's role in tango dancing. They also recognized women's intellectual capabilities in understanding the structure of the dance and their appreciation of the technical skills necessary for performing it at its best.

Bringing the wealth of oral knowledge that traditionally has been kept among friends and family into an organized written methodology takes a lot of effort, research, and actual experience. Being able to quantify, qualify, and further develop the valuable information acquired from the elders who witnessed and practiced the innovative aspects of the tango has been a rewarding journey for us. We hope that the fruits of that effort will be preserved as a source of reference for future generations. Regardless of how many styles develop and how much people may try to modify the tango dance, the structure of the dance based on the concept of *giros* (turns) will always be a fundamental point of reference for understanding changes and what's being changed.

A GIRO STATE OF MIND

When learning the basics in a vacuum, without the context of the reality of the dance floor, "sort of" dancing by connecting dots and going through the motions of memorized patterns, people tend to dance parallel to each other, leading and following their bodies into other dancers on the dance floor. Tango dancing is not an easy task, unless you fully understand the structure of the dance, are familiar with the fundamental concepts, and apply yourself to really learn rather than imitate. Many times you may feel that you are in the minority on the dance floor, but that is all right as long as you carry yourself with confidence and express the empowerment that knowledge provides.

Up until this point, you have worked to perfect the only three natural motions of each leg (opening, inside cross, and outside cross), to concentrate on three delicate placements of the feet on the floor (toe, sole, and heel), and to identify four distinctive body positions while traveling along the dance floor. The synergy resulting from the natural and logical confluence of movements and positions derives from a process called the eight-count giro, the embodiment of the tango dance. Think about the enjoyment and fun you'd sacrifice while trying to process each figure and each pattern, logging them in as a collection of steps in a vacuum and out of context. Instead, rejoice, because you are about to gain powerful knowledge of new body positions and to experience that smooth, elegant, sensual, passionate, playful, controlled, special state of mind, which we call a "giro state of mind."

Right Breast In

This position, as its name indicates, refers to the position of one partner's right breast in reference to the center of the chest of the other partner. It is found during the process of turning around each other. For the most part, the woman's right breast is aligned with the center of the man's chest. The right-breast-in position occurs on a clockwise turn when the woman steps forward with an inside cross of her right leg. The right-breast-in position occurs on a counterclockwise turn when the woman steps back with an outside cross of her left leg. On a clockwise turn (to the man's right), the position follows the woman's cruzada position (see figure 6.1):

1. The man marks the woman an inside cross with her right leg while he opens his right shoulder and extends either leg without weight change in front of the woman's left foot.

2. The woman responds to the mark by opening her right hip, turning her upper body to her right, and advancing her right leg in a circular trajectory around the man's axis.

Figure 6.1   Right-breast-in position.

On a counterclockwise turn (to the man's left), the position follows the salida position:

1. The man marks the woman an outside cross with her left leg while he opens his left shoulder and extends either leg without weight change to the inside edge of the woman's right foot.

2. The woman responds to the mark by opening her left hip, turning her upper body to her right, and stepping back with her left leg in a circular trajectory around the man's axis.

Left Breast In

This position, as its name indicates, refers to the position of one partner's left breast in reference to the center of the chest of the other partner. It is found during the process of turning around each other. For the most part, the woman's left breast is aligned with the center of the man's chest. The left-breast-in position occurs on a counterclockwise turn when the woman steps forward with an inside cross of her left leg. The left-breast-in position occurs on a clockwise turn when the woman steps back with an outside cross of her right leg. On a counterclockwise turn (to the man's left) the position follows the salida position (see figure 6.2):

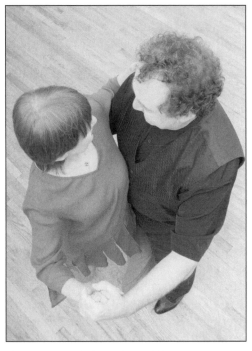

1. The man marks the woman an inside cross with her left leg while he opens his left shoulder and extends either leg without weight change in front of the woman's right foot.

2. The woman responds to the mark by opening her left hip, turning her upper body to her left, and advancing her left leg in a circular trajectory around the man's axis.

Figure 6.2 Left-breast-in position.

On a clockwise turn (to the man's right) the position follows the home position:

1. The man marks the woman an outside cross with her right leg while he opens his right shoulder and extends either leg without weight change to the inside edge of the woman's left foot.

2. The woman responds to the mark by opening her right hip, turning her upper body to her left, and stepping back with her right leg in a circular trajectory around the man's axis.

These two new body positions are essential for the proper execution of figures that involve giros, because they facilitate the intention of dancing around each other.

ANATOMY OF THE GIRO

A giro is a turning motion executed by the couple. In a giro, each dancer performs different functions. The woman uses the *cambio de frente*, or change of front, to move around the man. The man normally advances forward in a circular pattern into the woman's space. You'll remember that a change of front consists of three unique steps in the same direction: an inside cross and an outside cross linked by an opening. Also, in the case of the man walking forward in a circular pattern, he will cross with the inside leg and open with the outside leg. Make sure you understand this thoroughly before proceeding. If necessary, go back to the previous chapters and review.

The couple will have executed a complete eight-count giro when the woman has gone through two changes of front linked by a quick back step done on a quasi-circular trajectory. By definition, then, a *medio giro* (half a giro) is a movement where the woman executes only one cambio de frente. There are two major categories of giros. One happens when the man remains at the center of the woman's circular trajectory around him. The other one happens when the man steps into the woman's trajectory, trading places with her by moving into her space and displacing her into the space where he was.

A giro is a series of compound body positions in which the man initiates a movement and the woman continues the movement into the next position. Successful turning patterns require that the dancers change axis clearly, correctly, and timely to ensure the proper mix of balance and centrifugal force that is generated at the pivoting points. As is the case for every step of the dance, it is even more critical that the man learn how to mark every step of the giro according to the particular pattern he desires to execute. To recognize and respond flawlessly to the man's marks, the woman must allow herself to be moved from position to position. She must execute smooth transfers of weight and develop an instinctive sense of balance. She must understand her body positions in relationship to the man at every point of the code. This is, of course, easier said than done. But through the learning process we will break down each position of a giro into its components for both the man and woman.

An understanding of the structure of giros allows dancers to focus on the current moment with full knowledge and confidence that whatever comes next will happen within the realm of logic and common sense. The man will use his skills and understanding of the giro to improvise, entering and exiting at any of eight defined positions. Both the man and the woman will be able to reference every conceivable pattern or figure to sequences that contain elements of a giro.

Clockwise Eight-Count Giro

In a complete eight-count giro, the man executes eight steps, constantly turning to his right during the duration of the giro. Because the woman is always moving to his right side, the man's outside leg (the left in this case in a clockwise turn) cannot cross inside. It only opens forward. His inside leg (the right leg) always crosses inside as long as he is turning to his right. An interesting peculiarity of the eight-count giro is that the woman will actually step 10 times but use only eight changes of axis. In a full-count giro, the woman initiates three cambios de frente. The first complete change of front is done in a parallel system (dancers using opposite legs). The second complete change of front is done in cross-feet system (dancers using the same legs), and the third change of front is interrupted after the inside cross to end the giro. The two extra-quick steps are the back steps with the inside leg that follow the outside crosses and serve as a link from outside cross to inside cross.

An eight-count turn to the right, or clockwise, begins with the woman stepping forward to the man's right with an inside cross of her right leg and the man stepping forward into the woman's right side with an opening of his left leg. The end of la salida is a logical position in which to begin the clockwise eight-count turn. To set up for a clockwise giro, complete a simple salida. While the woman is locked with her left leg crossed in front of her right leg and her axis on her left in the cruzada position, the man needs to modify his position by crossing his right foot behind his left foot and bending his knees to allow his weight to be transferred to his right leg. Transferring the weight to his right leg allows his upper body to turn slightly to his right to begin opening his right shoulder and the path for the lady's first step of the giro. From this position, the steps proceed as follows (see figure 6.3 and figures 6.4 and 6.5 on pages 110 and 111):

Watch this demonstrated on the DVD

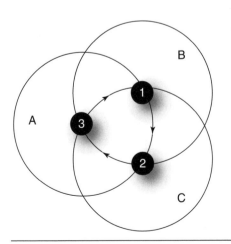

The woman steps forward from (1) to (2) on circle A, centered on the man's initial axis (3).

The man steps forward from (3) to (1) on circle C, centered on the woman's new axis (2).

The woman then steps laterally from (2) to (3) on circle B, centered on the man's new axis (1).

The man steps forward from (1) to (2) on circle A, centered on the woman's new axis (3).

The woman then steps backward from (3) to (1) on circle C, centered on the man's new axis (2).

The man steps forward from (2) to (3) on circle B, centered on the woman's new axis (1).

Figure 6.3   Trajectory of the eight-count giro con sacadas.

Clockwise giro 1.

1. The man unlocks the woman's legs by gently turning her on her left axis so she faces his right shoulder.

2. The woman responds by aligning her upper body so her right breast points to the center of the man's chest.

3. The man rotates gently to his right while pulling the lady down from her axis.

4. The woman responds by bending her support (left) leg and extending her right leg in a forward motion without changing axis. The woman's right leg begins to slide forward.

5. As the woman's right leg slides, the man extends his left leg forward in the direction of her right shoulder, placing his extended foot directly in front of or past the tip of her left shoe without changing axis (figure 6.4a).

6. With the upper bodies turning to the right, the woman's right arm is extended toward the man's left hand, and her left arm is extended toward the man's right shoulder.

Clockwise giro 2.

1. Still turning to his right, the man fully transfers his weight to his left leg, displacing the woman's body by bringing her to her right axis.

2. The woman responds by finishing her forward step, closing her left upper thigh slightly behind her right upper thigh so her right hip is ahead of her left hip and holding her left leg without weight.

3. As the man completes his weight transfer to his left leg, he makes a new axis, turning her body on her axis to the right with his body.

4. He releases his right arm, opening his right shoulder to mark the woman a forward step into the space where he was, trading places.

5. The woman responds by letting her body be turned on her axis and allowing her left leg to open into the space vacated by the man when he moved into her space, displacing her. Her left foot lands on the right side of the man.

6. He crosses his right leg toward her right shoulder, placing his right foot next to the inside edge of her right foot without changing weight. The bodies are now facing each other, with her right breast still aligned with the center of his chest (figure 6.4b).

Clockwise giro 3.

1. Without interruption, the man transfers his weight completely to his right leg and turns, making a new axis and bringing the woman to her left axis and turning her until her left breast is aligned with the center of his chest.

2. The woman responds by allowing her upper thighs to close, making a new axis on her left leg, and aligning her left breast with the center of his chest.

3. The man extends his right arm to release her body and lets her come down off her axis with an extension of her right leg.

4. He advances immediately with a forward step with his left leg, placing his foot next to the inner edge of her left shoe and keeping the center of his chest aligned with her left breast (figure 6.4c).

5. The man holds his axis completely on his left leg and holds a step either by tapping with his right leg extended behind or by simply pivoting on his left leg.

6. He opens his right arm to make the woman "fall" with a quick-step opening of her left leg to his right. This changes the system to cross feet.

7. The woman responds by not trying to bring herself to axis on her right but instead letting her body naturally "fall" into the empty space created by the man on his right side with a back opening of her inside (left) leg (figure 6.4d). Her right breast is once again aligned with the center of the man's chest.

Clockwise giro 4.

1. The man rotates farther to his right while pulling the lady down from her left axis.

2. The woman responds by bending her support (left) leg and extending her right leg in a forward motion without changing axis, exactly as she did in clockwise giro 1. The woman's right leg begins to slide forward.

3. As the woman's right leg slides forward, the man crosses his right leg forward in the direction of her right shoulder, placing his extended foot right in front of or past the tip of her left shoe without changing axis (figure 6.4e).

4. With the upper bodies turning to the right, the woman's right arm is once again extended toward the man's left hand, and her left arm is extended toward the man's right shoulder. Her right breast is pointing to the center of the man's chest.

Clockwise giro 5.

1. Still turning to his right, the man fully transfers his weight to his right leg, displacing the woman's body by bringing her to her right axis as in clockwise giro 2.

2. The woman responds by finishing her forward step, closing her left upper thigh slightly behind her right upper thigh, and holding her left leg without weight.

3. As the man completes his weight transfer to his right leg, he makes a new axis, turning her body on her axis to the right with his body as in clockwise giro 2.

4. He releases his right arm, opening his right shoulder to mark the woman a forward step into the space where he was and trading places as in clockwise giro 2.

5. The woman responds by letting her body be turned on her axis and allowing her left leg to open into the space vacated by the man when he moved into her space, displacing her as in clockwise giro 2. Her left foot lands on the right side of the man.

6. As her left foot lands on his right side, he extends his left leg forward in the direction of her right shoulder, placing his extended foot next to the inside edge of her left shoe without changing axis (figure 6.5a).

7. With the upper bodies turning to the right, the woman's right arm is extended toward the man's left hand, and her left arm is extended toward the man's right shoulder. The bodies are now facing each other with her right breast still aligned with the center of his chest.

Figure 6.4   Giro sequence in parallel system.

Clockwise giro 6.

1. Without interruption, the man transfers his weight completely to his left leg while still turning, making a new axis and bringing the woman to her left axis while turning her until her left breast is aligned with the center of his chest.

2. The woman responds by allowing her upper thighs to close, making a new axis on her left leg and aligning her left breast with the center of his chest.

3. The man extends his right arm to release her body and lets her come down off her axis with an extension of her right leg.

4. As her right leg lands on the ball of her foot, he advances forward immediately with his right leg over her left foot, placing his foot next to the inner edge of her left shoe (figure 6.5b) but keeping the center of his chest aligned with her left breast.

Figure 6.5 Giro sequence in cross-feet system.

5. He turns his upper body fully to his right, holding a step by pivoting on his right axis and opening his right arm to make the woman "fall" with a quick-step opening of her left leg to his right as in clockwise giro 3. This changes the system back to parallel feet.

6. The woman responds by not trying to bring herself to axis on her right leg but instead letting her body naturally "fall" into the empty space created by the man on his right side with a back opening of her inside (left) leg (figure 6.5c). Her right breast is aligned for the third time with the center of the man's chest.

Clockwise giro 7.

1. The man rotates farther to his right while pulling the lady down from her left axis.

2. The woman responds by bending her support (left) leg and extending her right leg in a forward motion without changing axis, exactly as she did in clockwise giro 1. The woman's right leg begins to slide forward.

3. As her right leg slides forward, he continues pivoting on his right axis, keeping the center of his chest aligned with her moving right breast until she finishes her forward step with her right leg. Then he opens his left leg to squarely straddle her, ending the rotation to the right (figure 6.5d). The woman's right arm is once again extended toward the man's left hand, and her left arm is extended toward the man's right shoulder. Her right breast is pointing to the center of the man's chest.

Clockwise giro 8.

1. The man stays in the open position with his weight evenly distributed and marks the woman a change of direction by turning her body clockwise on her right axis and holding her vertically.

2. The woman responds to the mark by letting her body be turned on her right axis, bringing her upper thighs together, and using her left arm to keep herself vertical without wobbling.

3. The man marks the woman an inside cross to his left side, changing his weight to his left leg.

4. The woman responds to the mark by extending her left leg toward the man's left shoulder and aligning her left breast with the center of his chest (figure 6.5e).

5. The man closes his right leg next to his left leg, transfers his weight in place to his right axis, and holds the woman on her left axis, turning her into him.

6. The woman responds to the mark by allowing herself to be brought to her left axis while placing her right foot behind her left foot to assume the cruzada position. Both dancers are now aligned as in the fourth step of la salida. Continue as you would from the end of a simple salida using what you have learned in the previous chapters.

This is the place where you want to spend plenty of time practicing and reviewing every position of the clockwise eight-count turn. Practice each stage of the entire sequence until the movements become smooth, synchronized, and under total control. The man is responsible for setting the pace and marking the woman's steps so that she responds effortlessly. The woman is responsible for allowing her body to be displaced and moved from axis to axis. She must overcome the desire to run the steps ahead of the mark. The woman must understand that the man begins to move her into a space that still has not been created but is being created as he changes his axis into her trajectory and places her where he was standing. In tango we trust.

Counterclockwise Eight-Count Giro

A powerful feature of the structure of the Argentine tango is the possibility of replicating on a left turn everything that is done on a right turn. The eight-count turn is no exception, although the starting and ending points of an eight-count giro to the left are different. The woman uses her left leg to alternate front and back crossings as required by the code. The man must keep his left arm tucked in, with his left hand as close as possible to his left shoulder to avoid having the woman pull away from him when she dances around him.

The setup for a counterclockwise eight-count giro to the left requires that the man begin by marking for the woman the first two steps of la base. The man quickly locks his left foot on the outside edge of the right shoe, crossing behind and bending his legs to change weight. The woman responds to the impulse by allowing her body to pass to the left side of the man with a back opening of her right leg.

Watch this demonstrated on the DVD

Counterclockwise giro 1.

1. The man continues turning to his left, tucking in his left arm and pulling the woman gently to his left. The woman responds by walking forward with her inside leg around the man while turning her upper body so that her left breast is aligned with the center of the man's chest. Her left shoulder opens to stay on the right shoulder of the man while her right shoulder extends to be on the left shoulder of the man. From the perspective of the man, her left leg now appears to be crossed in front of her right leg.

2. As the woman's left leg advances to the man's left, the man keeps his knees bent and extends his right leg in the opposite direction, placing his right foot in front of or past her right foot without changing weight.

Counterclockwise giro 2.

1. The man transfers his weight to his right leg, turning to his left and making the woman's upper body turn to the left on her left axis. She responds to the mark by finishing her step, letting the man turn her body on axis and keeping her left breast aligned with the center of the man's chest.

2. As the man completes his weight transfer to his right leg and makes a new axis, the rotation of his upper body makes the woman come down from her axis to his left side. She responds by letting her right leg open into the space vacated by the man as he's moving into her space, thus displacing her.

3. As the lady's right foot lands, the man extends his left leg, placing his foot next to the inside edge of her left foot without changing weight. Their bodies are now facing each other. The woman's right arm is bent at the elbow and square with her body, and the man's left breast is aligned with the center of the woman's chest.

Counterclockwise giro 3.

1. While holding the woman on her right axis, the man continues turning, shifts his weight to his left leg, and tucks his left arm. The woman responds by letting her left leg cross outside behind her right leg while keeping her left shoulder extended toward the man's right shoulder.

2. As she lands on the floor with the entire base (the entire forward side or edge of the inside of the foot) of her big toe, the man advances with his right leg, placing his foot next to the inner edge of her right shoe and aligning the center of his chest with the woman's right breast.

3. To continue the turn, the man releases the woman, extending his right shoulder, and pulls to his left with his left arm tucked against his shoulder. This allows the woman to end her outside cross with a double-step opening of her right leg.

4. The man holds a step either by tapping the foot of his left leg extended behind or by simply pivoting on his right leg. This changes the system to cross feet. Her left breast is once again pointing to the center of his chest.

Counterclockwise giro 4.

1. The woman is positioned again with her left side closer to the man, ready to initiate another change of front. That is, her axis is on her right leg, and she is poised to advance forward with an inside cross of her left to continue dancing around to the man's left side. The main difference between this position and counterclockwise giro 1 is that the man will extend his left leg, placing his left foot in front of her right foot without changing weight.

Counterclockwise giro 5.

1. The man transfers his weight to his left leg, turning to his left and making the woman's upper body turn on her left axis. She responds by bringing her right leg next to her left leg without putting weight on the right leg.

2. As the man completes his weight transfer to his left leg, making a new axis, the rotation of his upper body makes the woman come down from her axis. She responds by opening her right leg into the space vacated by the man when he moved into her space to displace her.

3. As the woman's right foot lands toward the man's left side, the man extends his right leg, placing his foot next to the inside edge of her left foot without changing weight. The bodies are now facing each other, the woman's right arm is bent at the elbow and square with her body, and the man's left breast is aligned with the center of the lady's chest.

Counterclockwise giro 6.

1. The man holds the woman on axis over her right leg while shifting his weight to his right leg and turning to his left. He then tucks his left arm and pulls the lady to his left side. The woman responds by letting her left leg cross outside behind her right leg while keeping her left shoulder extended toward the man's right shoulder.

2. As she lands on the floor with the base of her big toe, the man advances with his left leg over her right foot, placing his foot next to the inner edge of her right shoe and aligning the center of his chest with the woman's right breast.

3. To continue the turn, the man pivots on his left axis, releases the woman, extends his right shoulder, and pulls to his left with his left arm tucked against his shoulder. This allows the woman to end her outside cross with a double-step opening of her right leg. This changes the system to parallel feet. Her left breast is once again pointing to the center of his chest.

Counterclockwise giro 7.

1. The woman is positioned for the third time with her left side closer to the man, ready to step forward with an inside cross of her left leg. As the man marks her forward step, he continues pivoting on his left axis until she places her left foot on the floor.

2. Then he releases his right leg, opening laterally to straddle her, aligning her left breast to the center of his chest. This puts an end to the motion of the woman into the direction of the man's left shoulder.

Counterclockwise giro 8.

1. The man stays in the open position with his weight still on his left leg until the woman finishes shifting her weight completely to her left axis. Then he turns her upper body to change her direction, aligning her right breast with the center of his chest and pivoting half a turn to his left with both feet on the floor and weight on his left leg. The woman responds by allowing her body to turn on her left axis to change direction and aligning her right breast with the center of the man's chest.

2. The man marks a forward inside cross to his right side, shifting his weight to his right axis and stepping back with his left leg. The woman responds with an inside cross of her right leg. This position is identical to base 5 so the counterclockwise giro resolves finishing la base.

Practice these eight-count turns to the right and to the left as many times as it takes for both dancers to feel comfortable with the dynamics and with each other. When both dancers feel relaxed while going through the motions, try to link the two turns together by converting the seventh count in one direction (woman on a forward cross in front) into the first count in the other direction. This is done not by making the woman change direction in the eight-count turn but by keeping her going and converting the eight-count turn into the second count in the new direction. It sounds more complicated than it is, but a good understanding of the concepts just presented should allow both dancers to tackle the challenge. This is the objective of learning these concepts, because they will be used extensively as a blueprint in codifying and quantifying any possible combination you can think of.

Once the man learns the structure of the eight-count giro and is ready to apply all the concepts of marking and compliance with the code of the tango, we can concentrate on an endless series of partial turns that make use of the concepts already mastered. They are common navigational patterns based on improvisation—that is, dancing on the spur of the moment.

Medio Giro With Pasada

Watch this demonstrated on the DVD

This is one popular turn that uses half a giro and two displacements to create a tight passing 360-degree loop inserted between two salidas. It is possible to begin and end with the couple facing in the same direction. The use of displacements is important because it allows the couple to dance in tight spaces by trading places as they turn around each other rather than having the woman turn around the man, who stays at the center of her trajectory.

A *sacada*, or displacement, during a giro requires that the dancers move in opposite directions rather than the same direction. The principle of a sacada is for one dancer to move in the space left behind as the other dancer moves into the space left behind by the first dancer. In this example we will have the man displacing the woman by moving into her space and placing her in the space he leaves behind him as he moves into the woman's space.

The medio giro with pasada, also known as the 1-2-3 or top of the giro, begins from the cruzada position with a minor variant. On the fourth step of la salida, the man must cross his right foot behind his left foot, bending his knees and transferring his axis to the right leg. The toes must still be pointing out (the left at 10 o'clock and the right at 2 o'clock). The combination of crossing the right foot behind the left foot, keeping the toes pointed out, and bending the knees produces a natural rotation opening the right shoulder to indicate the direction of the turn for the woman (see figure 6.6).

Step 1. This is identical to clockwise giro 1. With his axis on his right leg tucked behind his left, the man marks the woman an inside cross to his right side with a gentle rotation of his upper body to his right. The woman responds to the mark by coming down from her left axis, extending her right leg forward while turning her upper body gently to her right toward him and aligning her right breast with the center of his chest. The man brings the lady to axis on her right leg and advances forward with his left leg, crossing the line between her legs and placing his shoe just ahead of her left leg. The ending position is the right-breast-in position (figure 6.6a).

Step 2. This is identical to clockwise giro 2. The man advances into the woman's space, changing weight to his left leg and turning to his right. He displaces the woman with his right arm by making her turn on her right axis and open laterally to his right. The woman responds by advancing her left leg in a forward motion, allowing her body to turn on her right axis, and letting her left leg open laterally in the direction of the man's right (rear) foot (figure 6.6b).

Step 3. This is identical to clockwise giro 3 except that after advancing into the woman's space, changing weight to his right leg, and displacing her, the man brings himself up to a full home position but with the center of his chest aligned with the left breast of the woman. Completing his clockwise rotation, the man walks forward, placing his left shoe next to the inner edge of her left shoe. He extends his right arm to allow the woman to come down from her axis, extending her right leg on an outside cross. The woman responds by stepping back with her right leg, making solid contact on the floor with the entire base (using the entire inside and forward edge of the foot) of her big toe, disassociating her hips from her upper body, and assuming the left-breast-in position (figure 6.6c). The man keeps his right arm tucked in so that there is no space for the woman to come down from her back step to his right side. This ends the turning movement to the right of the man.

The man creates a change of direction for the woman by passing over to the woman's right side with a forward motion of his right leg. She responds by allowing her axis to be transferred to her back (right) leg and her body to turn on her right axis so her left leg now crosses outside behind her right

Figure 6.6 Giro with pasada sequence (counted as 1-2-3).

leg to the left side of the man. Both dancers assume the outside right position. You should recognize this position as the second step of la base and la salida. The medio giro con pasada resolves, completing la salida at the cruzada position.

On the woman's first two steps, the man is on her right side; but on her third step, when she changes front, he finds himself on her left side. In other words, the woman rolls across his torso, first aligning her right breast on the center of his chest on her first step, aligning the center of her chest with his right breast on her second step, and finally aligning her left breast with the center of his chest on her third step. The man must be aware of this body alignment to make sure he is on her left side when he steps with his left leg on the third movement, making it obvious that he needs to pass to her right side to end the clockwise pattern. He changes the direction of the trajectory into a salida, which is a counterclockwise pattern.

Medio Giro in Cross-Feet System

Watch this demonstrated on the DVD To change to a cross-feet system, the man will double-step on the first step of la base, closing with his right with a change of axis while holding the lady on her right axis. This medio giro will start with an outside back cross of the woman, followed by an inside quick opening and ending with an inside forward cross (see figure 6.7).

From the home position, the man marks the first step of la base. While holding the woman on her right axis, the man closes with his right foot, changing his weight to his right leg. The man marks the second step of la base for the woman while stepping forward on a left diagonal with his left leg. The woman responds to the mark by executing an outside cross with her left leg. The man transfers his weight completely to his left leg, bringing the woman to her left axis and beginning to turn to his right, turning her until her left breast is aligned with the center of his chest.

Figure 6.7 Cross-feet clockwise medio giro (counted as 6-&-7-8).

Step 1. This step is identical to clockwise giro 6. The man steps forward with his right leg toward the woman's left breast, releasing the embrace so she can extend her right leg on an outside cross to the right, and placing his right foot over her left foot next to its inner edge (figure 6.7a). As he shifts his weight to his right leg, the man continues to turn his upper body to his right, opening his right arm. The woman responds by allowing her inside leg to open backward into the man's right, making axis on her left leg. This extra-quick step of the woman while he holds a step returns the couple to the parallel system (figure 6.7b).

Step 2. This movement is identical to clockwise giro 7. While still turning to the right on his right axis, the man marks an inside forward cross for the woman into his rear leg. The woman responds to the mark by extending her right leg to execute an inside forward cross. As soon as the woman's right foot lands on the floor, the man stops the turn by extending his left leg, opening to his left, and straddling the woman's inside cross (figure 6.7c). He brings her up to her right axis and turns her body to point to his left shoulder. She responds by allowing her body to turn on axis, closing her thighs, and keeping her left leg from advancing.

Step 3. This movement is identical to clockwise giro 8. The man shifts his weight to his left leg and marks for the woman an inside forward cross, which she executes with her left leg. The man brings the woman to her left axis while closing with his right leg (figure 6.7d). As he changes weight to his right axis, the man turns the woman's body into him with weight change, turning her body to assume the cruzada position. The woman responds by allowing her body to turn on her left axis, assuming the cruzada position. This medio giro, which is also known as the 6-7-8 or the bottom of the giro because of the obvious use of the last three movements of the eight-count giro, resolves forward to the man's left with a resolution, base, or cambio de frente.

The Half Moon

This is one of the oldest tango figures adapted to our contemporary view of the dance. The name describes the trajectory on which the woman travels as she walks three steps to his right and three steps to his left, drawing half a circle around the man. First we execute a *media luna*, as the half moon is known in the tango circles, from the cruzada position. To set up for a half moon, start a simple salida ending at the cruzada position. The man has the choice to start the half moon in parallel system and change to cross-feet system on the third step or to start the half moon in cross-feet system. We prefer to start it in cross-feet system. The man holds his axis on his left leg without changing axis to his right.

Watch this demonstrated on the DVD

Step 1. The man marks for the woman an inside forward cross identical to clockwise giro 4 while he receives her step with a back opening of his inside (right) leg. The woman responds to the mark by executing an inside forward cross with her right leg, assuming the right-breast-in position (see figure 6.8a).

Step 2. The man marks a forward step for the outside (left) leg of the woman, identical to clockwise giro 5. She responds to the mark with a forward opening of her left leg toward the man. The man receives her step with an outside cross of his left leg as he begins to turn to his right. In shorthand, the woman does a side step while the man does a back step (figure 6.8b).

Step 3. The man marks an outside back cross for the right leg of the woman by turning her body with his body. She responds to the mark in an identical manner as in clockwise giro 6, extending her right leg on an outside cross behind her left leg while assuming the left-breast-in position. The man receives her outside back cross with an opening of his right leg to his right, straddling her with a side step while she is on a back step (figure 6.8c).

Step 4. The man shifts axis completely to his right and brings the woman up on her right axis, gently pulling her right shoulder with his left arm to make her turn on her right axis. The woman responds to the mark by allowing herself to be brought on axis and turned, assuming the right-breast-in position. The

Figure 6.8 Half moon.

man rotates his body to his left and marks an outside back cross of her left leg. The woman responds to the mark by executing an outside cross with her left leg. The man receives her outside cross by shifting his weight to his left leg (figure 6.8d).

Step 5. The man turns farther to his left, marking an inside back opening of the woman's right leg. She responds to the mark by letting her right leg open, going back to the man's left side. The man receives the inside back opening of her right leg by advancing with an inside cross of his right leg (figure 6.8e).

Step 6. The man holds the next step while marking for the woman an inside back cross of her left leg with a gentle push of his upper body. The woman responds by executing an inside back cross of her left leg, assuming the cruzada position (figure 6.8f).

As the woman returns to her initial position, the man resolves in the forward direction, making a decision whether to resume la base, to end with a resolution, or to link into a change of front.

It is up to the man to define the length and radius of the woman's trajectory. The less the man moves, using short steps in a circular trajectory, the tighter the woman's half moon will be. Conversely, the more the man moves, the looser her half moon will be.

The change of direction for the woman takes place with two consecutive back steps linked with a pivot. The combined action of the cross behind to the right of the man, the pivot on axis, and the cross behind to the left side of the man is a figure known as *back ocho* because as the woman executes the movement, her feet seem to be drawing a number 8 (ocho) on the floor. This sequence can be repeated a number of times, changing the lady's direction after each back step, and moving to the edge of the dance floor before finishing the original pattern.

In this chapter we have introduced the concepts of giros and sacadas—that is, turning and displacing by virtue of trading places as you dance around each other. The eight-count giro is a structure that contains all the elements of the tango. We have learned that popular figures like forward and back ochos are not isolated steps to be learned, but rather direction changes, where an inside cross follows an inside cross or an outside cross follows an outside cross after the body turns on axis, changing the relative positions of the legs with respect to the partner. In the next two chapters we introduce popular figures that are among the options available to the man in terms of trajectories and patterns to circulate around the floor in an orderly and pleasant fashion. It is very important that you not overlook the contents of this chapter because you will use these concepts throughout the rest of your learning process. Spend some time practicing and thoroughly understanding the body positions and alignments associated with the eight-count giro, and become proficient in the two examples of medio giros and the half moon (media luna) figures.

CHAPTER 7

A Sleight of Legs

Let's dance, girlfriend, the people are watching. Let's dance this tango, embraced really close, with only one soul between the two of us.

—*"Tango bailemos"*: Pascual Mamone, composer; Reinaldo Yiso, lyricist

*I*n this chapter, you apply everything you have learned so far to develop a solid concept of improvisation—to dance on the spur of the moment in response to the dynamics of the dance floor, the action of other dancers, and the music. Concepts such as the code of the tango and the eight-count giro are the blueprints for figures and patterns that help you sort out the unexpected changes of condition that occur on any dance floor.

As you enter the dance floor, remember that the woman dances around the man and the man dances around the floor. This now becomes more obvious and important, because in order for the dancers to do that with ease and enjoyment, they need to understand why they change directions, when to change directions, and how to change directions. Changing directions while traveling along the dance floor creates a mesmerizing intertwining of legs, which is what everyone notices right away. In this chapter you will continue to learn how to create the illusion of the tango with a clever and well-understood sleight of legs.

The use of the phrase *change of direction* in the context of dancing tango refers to the trajectory that the woman follows as she dances around the man. Her intention must always be to dance around the man, either to his left side or to his right side. She must never "follow" by stepping back away from or stepping forward into the man. The man changes the direction of the woman, and she moves to the opposite side of the man. She needs to understand and be aware of which side of the man she is on so that she can resolve his marks to continue on the same side or move to the opposite side. That is, she must keep moving in the same direction until the man changes her direction. She then begins to move in the opposite direction. The woman's path often intersects the man's path.

TRADITIONAL CHANGES OF DIRECTION

We use the adjective *traditional* to define time-honored, accepted, and popular practices used during the period known as the golden years. We use that period as a point of reference for the quality and authenticity of our dancing. The preservation, fostering, and perpetuation of classical forms in the tango are what give it the feel and look that make it the unadulterated Argentine tango.

At the core of the classical dance are three traditional ways of changing the direction of the woman as she dances around the man. Each change of direction can take place at one of the three steps of the code of the tango: the inside forward cross, the lateral opening, and the outside back cross.

The characteristic of these traditional changes of direction is that the woman repeats the same step of the code she used to stop traveling in one direction in order to begin traveling in the opposite direction. For example, if she is dancing to the right of the man and stepping forward with an inside cross of her right leg, a change of her direction to the man's left will have her pivoting clockwise on her right axis and stepping to the man's left with a forward inside cross of her left leg. The resulting figure is what is commonly known as a forward ocho, because with a little imagination you can see a number 8 drawn on the floor by the fanning action of her legs.

Similarly, if the woman is dancing to the left of the man and stepping back with an outside cross of her left leg, a change of her direction to the man's right will have her pivoting clockwise on her left axis and stepping to the man's right with an outside cross of her right leg. The resulting figure is commonly known as a back ocho.

Finally, if the woman is in the process of opening her left leg as she dances to the right of the man, a change of her direction to the man's left will have her put weight on her left axis and quickly change it to her right axis with a rocking motion to begin moving to the man's left side with an opening of her right leg. This form of changing directions along the lady's openings is part of a grouping commonly known as *arrepentidas*. These are sudden, evasive stop-and-return rocking movements used primarily as a way to avoid a collision and most likely as a way to dance on one tile in tight spaces where advancing is almost impossible.

arrepentida—A change of mind. Evasive actions that allow a couple to back away from a collision or traffic jam in a minimal amount of space and on short notice.

Forward Ochos

Most forward ochos, or *ochos adelante* as native tango teachers sometimes call them, begin to the right side of the man and end to the left side of the man, although there is no reason not to reverse the process. The first step of a forward ocho for the woman is a replication of her clockwise giro 1 or clockwise giro 4 body positions (right breast in) that the man receives in a variety of ways to create different looks. The second step of a forward ocho is a replication of her counterclockwise giro 1 or counterclockwise giro 4 body positions (left breast in) that the man receives in a variety of ways to create different looks. Forward ochos typically start from the cruzada position, from the home position on base 4, or from the inside forward cross of the clockwise or counterclockwise giro.

Let's start with forward ochos from the cruzada position (see figure 7.1). The setup is the execution of a simple salida. Upon reaching the cruzada position at the end of the salida, the man may stay in place (stationary ochos), or he may move along (walking ochos) in parallel or cross-feet systems. To use the parallel system, the man will close with his right with a weight shift at the cruzada position. Conversely, to change to the cross-feet system, the man will close with his right without weight change at the cruzada position. Forward ochos that start to the right of the man resolve to the left of the man with a resolution, change of front, or la base.

As improvisation skills continue to develop, it will become more obvious that the look of any figure, a figure eight in this case, can be easily altered by having the man accompany the woman's motion in different ways. Here are three possibilities: placing his right foot a half a step behind his left foot, closing the right leg with weight change, and closing the right leg without weight change.

Stationary Forward Ocho

Step 1. Upon reaching the cruzada position at the end of the salida, the man brings his right foot halfway, rather than completely, to a close. He unlocks her right leg with a slight rotation to his left and brings her down from her axis with a gentle rotation to his right, transferring his weight to his right leg and pulling gently with his right arm while keeping her right shoulder extended with his left arm. The woman responds by executing an inside forward cross with her right leg.

> Watch this demonstrated on the DVD

Step 2. The man brings the woman up on her right axis and rotates her body on axis so her left breast is pointing to the center of his chest.

Step 3. The man transfers his weight back to his left leg, opening his left shoulder and marking an inside cross of her left leg. The woman responds with an inside forward cross, assuming the left-breast-in position.

Step 4. The man receives her forward step by closing with his right leg, transferring his weight to his right axis, and bringing her up on her left axis turning her to face him. The woman responds by allowing her axis to be shifted, allowing her body to be turned on axis, and assuming the cruzada position.

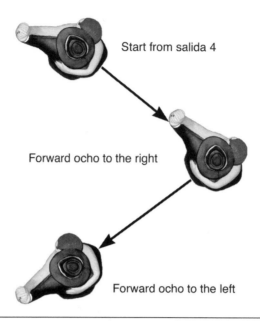

Start from salida 4

Forward ocho to the right

Forward ocho to the left

Figure 7.1 The trajectory of a forward ocho.

Forward Ocho in Parallel System

Watch this demonstrated on the DVD

Step 1. The man unlocks the right leg of the woman with a slight rotation to his left and brings her down from her axis with a gentle rotation to his right, pulling gently with his right arm while keeping her right shoulder extended with his left arm. The woman responds by executing an inside forward cross with her right leg.

Step 2. The man receives the woman's inside cross by stepping back with an outside cross of his left leg, closing his right leg without axis change, and bringing the woman up on her right axis while rotating her upper body into his right shoulder. The woman responds by finishing her forward step, allowing her body to rotate while staying on axis, and aligning her left breast with the center of the man's chest.

Step 3. The man rotates his upper body gently to his left, marking an inside forward cross of her left leg by extending her right arm and gently accompanying with his right arm. The woman responds by executing an inside forward cross with her left leg.

Step 4. The man receives the woman's inside cross by shifting his weight to his right axis and bringing the woman up on her left axis while rotating her upper body into his left shoulder. The woman responds by transferring her weight to her left leg, allowing her body to rotate on her axis to face the man, and hooking her right leg behind the left leg to assume the cruzada position.

Forward Ocho in Cross-Feet System

Step 1. The man, standing on his left axis, unlocks the right leg of the woman with a slight rotation to his left and brings her down from her axis, pulling her gently with his right arm straight into his body while opening back with his right leg. The woman responds by executing an inside forward cross with her right leg into the space vacated by his right leg.

Watch this demonstrated on the DVD

Step 2. The man receives the woman's inside cross by making an axis on his right leg, closing his left leg without weight change, and bringing the woman up on her right axis. The woman responds by finishing her forward step, allowing her body to rotate while staying on axis, and aligning her left breast with the center of the man's chest.

Step 3. The man opens his left shoulder to make room for the lady to advance with her inside (left) leg. The man pulls the woman's right shoulder gently with his left arm to bring her into his left side while holding her left shoulder in firm contact with his right shoulder. The woman responds by assuming the left-breast-in position and executing an inside cross with her left leg. This position resembles the letter X because her legs and shoulders are in a counterposition. As her left leg extends forward, her left shoulder stays back while her right shoulder goes forward as a result of the rotation of her upper body toward the man. The man opens laterally to receive the woman's inside forward cross.

Step 4. While the woman is changing axis to her left leg, the man brings his right leg to close with weight change, holding her on her left axis with his right arm while gently pulling her around with his left arm to have her facing him. She responds by allowing her body to be turned in toward the man and assuming the cruzada position.

Forward Ocho From la Base

The setup for a forward ocho sequence from la base occurs on the fourth step of la base (base 4), when the man opens to his right with his right leg and brings the woman to her left axis. The actual forward ocho begins with the fifth step of la base (base 5) as the man marks an inside forward cross for the woman by extending his right arm slightly to prevent the woman from going into his right side. What follows is identical to forward ochos in parallel system (see figure 7.2).

Watch this demonstrated on the DVD

Step 1. This is the same as base 5.

Step 2. As the woman executes an inside forward step assuming the outside right position, the man receives her inside cross by stepping back with an outside cross of his left leg, shifting his weight to his left axis, and bringing the woman up on her right axis while rotating her upper body into his right shoulder. The woman responds by finishing her forward step, allowing her body to rotate while staying on axis, and aligning her left breast with the center of the man's chest.

Step 3. The man marks an inside forward cross to his left, which she executes by advancing with her left leg. As she is stepping to his left, the man turns to his left, opening his right leg around her right axis. He closes with his left leg without changing weight.

Step 4. After the woman completes her change of axis to her left, they turn to face each other. The man steps forward with his left leg, repeating the sequence until he resolves forward with a resolution.

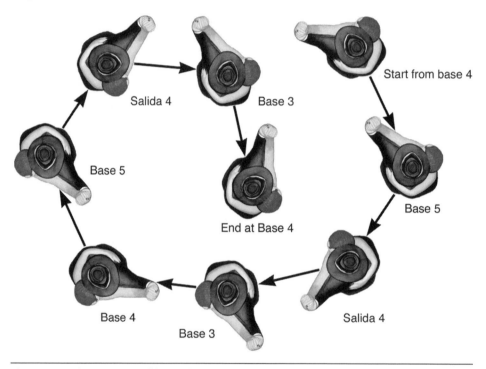

Salida 4　　　Base 3　　Start from base 4

Base 5

End at Base 4　　Base 5

Base 4　　Base 3　　Salida 4

Figure 7.2　The trajectory of forward ochos from la base.

Forward Ocho From a Giro

A forward ocho serves the purpose of changing the direction in which the woman is moving around the man. Therefore, in the process of executing a clockwise eight-count giro, there are three positions when a forward ocho may be used to end the progress of the woman into the right side of the man. They are clockwise giro 1, clockwise giro 4, and clockwise giro 7 when the woman is advancing with an inside cross of her right leg.

Step 1. Initiate clockwise giro 1 (parallel system) or clockwise giro 4 (cross-feet system).

Step 2. In parallel system (clockwise giro 1), the man advances with a forward opening of his left leg, transferring his weight forward to his left axis and displacing her but holding her on her right axis without turning his body. In cross-feet system (clockwise giro 4), the man advances with a forward inside cross of his right leg, transferring his weight forward to his right axis and displacing her but holding her on her right axis without turning his body. The woman allows her body to be turned on her right axis to assume the position of dancing around the man's left side.

Step 3. In parallel system (clockwise giro 1), the man waits on his left axis and marks an inside cross of her left leg. The woman responds by stepping with an inside forward cross. The man brings his right leg to a close, changing weight and turning the woman to face him. The woman assumes the cruzada position. In cross-feet system (clockwise giro 4), the man waits for the woman to step with her left leg. After she assumes the cruzada position, he resolves walking forward with his left leg to a standard resolution.

Back Ocho

A back ocho is a figure that results when a change of direction takes place on the outside cross or back step of the change of front. In concept, the back ocho is identical to the forward ocho, except the woman executes outside crosses from one side of the man to the other, allowing her body to be turned on axis in between outside crosses (see figure 7.3). The man must be aware that to step with her outside leg, the woman needs to disassociate her upper body from her hips and extend her leg from the hip to reach into his other side. The line of the woman's upper body does not vary when doing back ochos. To avoid the possibility of separating during back ochos, the man uses forward openings to receive her outside crosses. So, generally, back ochos are done in cross-feet system.

The first step of a back ocho for the woman is a replication of her counterclockwise giro 3 or clockwise giro 6 body positions (right breast in) that the man receives with a forward opening of his left leg. The second step of a back ocho is a replication of her clockwise giro 3 or counterclockwise giro 6 body positions (left breast in) that the man receives with a forward opening of his right leg. Back ochos typically start on the second step of la base (base 2) or from the outside back cross of the clockwise or counterclockwise giro.

Back Ocho in Cross-Feet System

Step 1. To set up for back ochos, start with base 1. While holding the woman on her right axis, the man closes his right leg and shifts weight to change to cross-feet system.

Watch this demonstrated on the DVD

Step 2. The man marks the woman an outside cross of her left leg by bringing her diagonally to his left with an opening of his left leg, transferring his weight, and holding her on her left axis. The woman responds by extending her left leg in the direction the man is taking her, allowing her hips to create the right-breast-in position, and finishing the back step on the new axis.

Step 3. The man changes direction to his right with his right leg, pushing gently on the woman's right shoulder and bringing her diagonally to his right, transferring his weight, and holding her on her right axis. The woman responds by allowing her left hip to turn so her right leg can pass, crossing outside in the direction the man is taking her, and assuming the left-breast-in position.

Step 4. The man repeats step 1 to bring the woman back to his left. He either repeats step 2 to continue with the back ochos or resolves with a cross-feet salida.

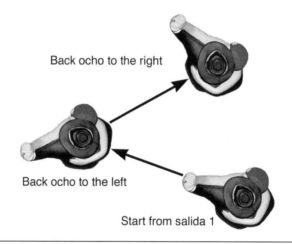

Back ocho to the right

Back ocho to the left

Start from salida 1

Figure 7.3 The trajectory of a back ocho.

Back Ocho From a Giro

Watch this demonstrated on the DVD

A back ocho serves the purpose of changing the direction in which the woman is moving around the man. Therefore, in the process of executing a clockwise eight-count giro, there are two positions when a back ocho may be used to end the progress of the woman into the right side of the man. They are clockwise giro 3 and clockwise giro 6, when the woman is backing into the right side of the man with an outside cross of her right leg.

Step 1. After clockwise giro 2, the man transfers his weight to his right leg, displacing the woman, rotating to his right, and holding her on her left axis. She responds by allowing her body to be displaced, rotated, and held on axis while she brings her legs together without weight change.

Step 2. The man double-steps by closing with his left leg and opening to his right with his right leg while marking an outside cross for the woman across his opening. She responds by executing an outside cross with her right leg and assuming the left-breast-in position.

Step 3. The man brings his left leg together, holding his axis on his right while turning the woman's body away from him to mark an outside cross to his left. She responds by allowing her body to turn on her right axis. The man brings the woman to his left, opening his left shoulder. She responds by extending her left leg in an outside cross and assuming the right-breast-in position.

Forward and back ochos are essential changes of direction for dancers who strive to achieve improvisational excellence. Because the woman dances around the man executing the code of the tango, the man is presented with the opportunity to launch into ochos on every other one of her steps when she is crossing inside or outside.

Arrepentida

The third traditional way to change directions occurs during the openings for the lady (see figure 7.4). It is a quick, evasive movement (arrepentida) for avoiding collisions with other dancers. In fact, the whole purpose of its execution was the result of extremely crowded conditions on dance floors, where there was no room to complete an opening or continue with an outside cross. As the tango of the milongueros of Buenos Aires began to replace the acrobatic feats of the stage dancers, a collection of arrepentidas quickly became a subset of moves. There is no certainty about the first time somebody confused the interruption of the open step of the giro with the falling off axis in a badly executed forward ocho and named the interruption of the giro *ocho cortado* (cut ocho).

Interrupting la Salida

A typical interruption of la salida occurs on salida 3. The resulting change of direction resolves into base 5 with a 90-degree turn to the man's right.

Watch this demonstrated on the DVD

Step 1. Start with salida 1 and continue with salida 2.

Step 2. The man begins execution of salida 3 by advancing with his left leg on a diagonal to his left. The woman responds by opening in a diagonal backward with her inside (right) leg. But wait! Let's say that we want to interrupt the progress of the movement and change directions.

Step 3. The man stops his forward motion, quickly changing his weight back to his right leg, bringing his right foot a half step behind his left foot, and relaxing his right arm to make the woman place her full weight back on her right leg and then quickly rebound back so her weight transfers forward to her left leg.

Step 4. The man retraces his path to where he was coming from, but he begins to turn to his right, opening his left leg to the back. The woman responds by retracing her path, executing base 5 with an inside forward cross of her right leg, and assuming the outside right position.

Step 5. The man now turns completely to his right, using a lateral opening of his right leg. The woman responds with an opening of her left leg, assuming the clockwise giro 2 position. But wait! There is no room to continue with an outside cross of her right leg—other dancers' legs and feet are in the way. So what can resourceful tango dancers do? Whether there is actually another obstacle looming to the right or just because the dancers know very well the concept of direction changes, everyone watching thinks it is an interesting move when . . .

Step 6. The man quickly rocks back to his left axis and brings the woman left to right, turning slightly to his left to make her left leg cross inside over her right. She responds by allowing her weight to be changed quickly, keeping both feet on the ground, and rotating her right hip to the left to make room for the inside cross of her left leg. The man receives the crossing of her feet, bringing his right leg to a close with a change of axis.

Interrupting la Base

Watch this demonstrated on the DVD A typical interruption of la base occurs on base 3, and the resulting change of direction converts to base 6 and resolves into base 1 with a 90-degree turn to the man's left.

Step 1. Start with base 1 and continue with base 2.

Step 2. The man begins execution of base 3, advancing with his left leg in front of his right foot. The woman responds by opening in a diagonal backward with her inside (right) leg. But wait! Somebody just stopped in front of you, or worse, you and your partner are in the path of a couple heading your way on a collision course. So what are learned tango dancers to do?

Step 3. The man stops his forward motion, quickly changing his weight back to his right leg, bringing his right foot a half step behind his left foot, and relaxing his right arm to make the woman place her full weight back on her right leg and then quickly rebound back so her weight transfers forward to her left leg.

Step 4. The man retraces his path to where he was coming from, but he turns to his left, opening with his left leg to execute base 1. The woman responds by retracing her path, executing base 1 with an opening of her right leg and assuming the salida position. The couple has a variety of options in proceeding from here.

Try an interesting combination beginning with the interruption of the salida followed by step 2 of the interruption of la base. The result is that a salida and a resolution have been replaced by linking their interruptions into a different pattern. Judicious use of improvisational skills matching the rhythm of the music allows for an effective way to dance when space is at a premium.

The concept of quick changes of direction using evasive moves becomes part of the reaction mechanism of the body and is triggered by the rhythm of the

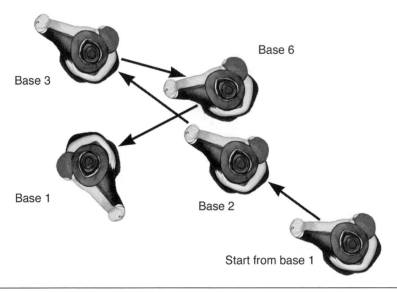

Figure 7.4 The trajectory of an arrepentida to interrupt la base.

music. In fact, the interpretation of the rhythm when using arrepentidas sounds something like this: "step-and-step," or "one-and-two," or "forward-and-backward," or "back-and-forward," or "side-and-side," or "quick-quick-slow."

NONTRADITIONAL CHANGES OF DIRECTION

To understand what is meant by nontraditional changes of direction, you need to make sure that you understand the concept of changes of direction as they relate to the woman's direction when she dances around the man. As she dances around the man, she is in "giro mode," whether actually going through an entire sequence or just a segment of it.

The man generally is at the center of the woman's trajectory, effectively in an inner spot, lane, or line, while he makes her travel on an outside line, track, or lane. If the giro includes sacadas (displacements), the man moves into the outer track while displacing the lady to the inner track, changing the track where he stands as the inner track and the track where she stands as the outer track.

Nevertheless, the giro itself tends to be stationary (that is, the couple occupies a space on the dance floor and executes the turning pattern before moving along the dance floor). So if a giro to the right is being executed, a change of direction results in a giro to the left and vice versa. Changes of direction use the same step of the code to end a giro in one direction and start a giro in another direction.

During the 1990s, dancers began to alter the traditional methods of changing the direction of a giro by moving the axis of the giro as well. Instead of making the woman go around the man, the man goes around the woman on one of the three steps of her code to change the center axis of her circular trajectory. These alterations result in each direction of the giro having a different center of rotation for the woman. The effect is one of a traveling giro rather than the traditional stationary giro. For example, if the woman is on the back step of the code crossing a leg outside behind the support leg, and the man moves close to her crossed foot sharing her axis, he blocks the back opening of her inside leg. If he turns in the opposite direction, he changes the direction of the giro by having the woman turn on her axis into him instead of away from him as she would turn for a figure eight (ocho) and begin the giro in a new direction and around a different center.

In the traditional figure eight, the trailing feet draw the shape of the number eight on the floor as they come around the turn into the new direction, whereas here the resulting drawing resembles a pie slice. Imagine the leg crossing outside at the center of a pie. The other leg draws the edge or the base of the slice as she turns into the man. There are a total of four main alterations, two for the inside crosses and two for the outside crosses.

1. From inside cross to the right to outside cross to the left
2. From inside cross to the left to outside cross to the right
3. From outside cross to the right to inside cross to the left
4. From outside cross to the left to inside cross to the right

The first two alterations allow a change of direction from a forward ocho in one direction to a back ocho in the opposite direction, while the last two allow a change of direction from a back ocho in one direction to a forward ocho in the opposite direction. In other words, the alterations allow changes of direction from the inside cross of a giro in one direction to the outside cross of a giro in the opposite direction and vice versa. Since the woman alternates inside and outside crosses when dancing around the man, the possibilities of using alterations add to the power of improvisation of the dancers.

Alteration Forward Right to Back Left

Watch this demonstrated on the DVD

To set up for this change of direction, begin a forward ocho sequence in cross-feet system. This is commonly started from the cruzada position at the end of the salida. Start with salida 1; continue with salida 2, salida 3, and salida 4. The man closes with his right leg, holding his axis on his left to change to cross-feet system. See its trajectory in figure 7.5.

Step 1. With his weight on his left axis, the man marks the beginning of a forward ocho. The woman responds by advancing forward with her inside (right) leg. The man receives her inside cross with the right side of his chest by intersecting her trajectory with an opening of his right leg. The woman responds by allowing her forward motion to come to a rest on the man's chest.

Step 2. As he intersects her path, the man comes up into his right axis, holding her up on her right axis, turning to his left side, and opening his left shoulder. The woman responds by finishing her forward step, staying on axis, and allowing her body to turn to her left.

Step 3. The man comes down from his axis, extending his left leg in a back diagonal opening to his left, and pulling the woman's right arm gently but firmly to bring her to his left side. The woman responds by extending her left leg, crossing it back into the man's left side, and assuming the right-breast-in position.

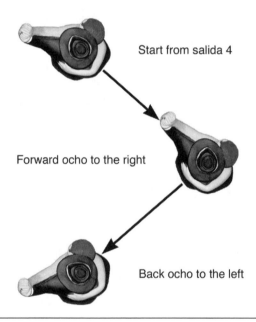

Start from salida 4

Forward ocho to the right

Back ocho to the left

Figure 7.5　The trajectory of an alteration forward right to back left.

This movement resembles a back ocho, and indeed it is. The fact that the woman is stepping backward with an outside cross is the result of the setup and the transition from a forward ocho. Resolving into a back ocho sequence is a common option to continue dancing.

The position also resembles counterclockwise giro 6 for the woman. The man may resolve by locking his right foot behind his left leg, changing weight, and turning to his left. This action marks a back opening for the woman's inside leg, resulting in the woman's changing axis to her right leg and presenting her left side to the man. The man is now ready to advance with his left leg and displace the woman as in counterclockwise giro 4.

Alteration Forward Left to Back Right

Watch this demonstrated on the DVD

To set up for this change of direction, complete a forward ocho sequence in cross-feet system. This is conveniently started from the cruzada position at the end of the salida. Start with salida 1; continue with salida 2, salida 3, and salida 4. The man closes with his right leg, holding his axis on his left to change to cross-feet system. The trajectory is shown in figure 7.6.

Step 1. With his weight on his left axis, the man marks the beginning of a forward ocho. The woman responds by advancing forward with her inside (right) leg. The man receives her inside cross with a back opening of his right leg, brings her up on her right axis, and rotates her to face his left side.

Step 2. With the weight on his right axis, the man marks the ending of the forward ocho. The woman responds by advancing forward with her inside (left) leg. The man receives her inside cross with the left side of his chest by moving into her left axis with an opening of his left leg. The woman responds by allowing her forward motion to come to a rest on the man's chest.

Step 3. As he intersects her path, the man comes up into his left axis, holding her up on her left axis, turning to his right side, and opening his right shoulder. The woman responds by finishing her forward step, staying on axis, and allowing her body to turn to her right.

Step 4. The man comes down from his axis, extending his right leg in a back diagonal opening to his right, and pulling the woman gently but firmly to bring her to his right side. The woman responds by extending her right leg, crossing it back into the man's right side, and assuming the left-breast-in position.

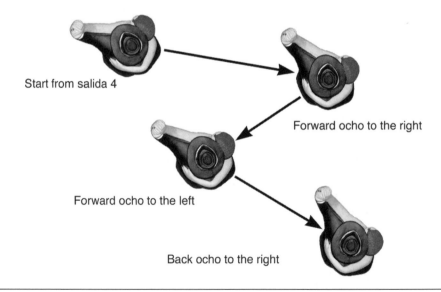

Start from salida 4

Forward ocho to the right

Forward ocho to the left

Back ocho to the right

Figure 7.6 The trajectory of an alteration forward left to back right.

This movement resembles a back ocho, and indeed it is. The fact that the woman is advancing by stepping backward with an outside cross is the result of the setup and the transition from a forward ocho. So resolving into a back ocho sequence is a common option to continue dancing.

The position also resembles clockwise giro 6 for the woman. The man may resolve by locking his left foot behind his right leg, changing weight, and turning to his right. This action marks a back opening for the woman's inside leg, resulting in the woman's changing axis to her left leg and presenting her right side to the man. The man now is ready to advance with his right leg and displace the woman as in clockwise giro 4.

Alteration Back Right to Forward Left

This change of direction begins on an outside cross of the woman's right leg to the man's right and ends with an inside forward cross of her left leg to the man's left. The man uses diagonal openings in cross-feet system to receive the woman's crosses. Here is a common application of this change of direction (trajectory is shown in figure 7.7):

Watch this demonstrated on the DVD

Step 1. The man marks salida 1 to the woman, but he stays on her left side by stepping short with his left leg, closing his right leg, and changing weight to enter the cross-feet system. The woman responds by assuming the salida position and holding her axis on her right leg.

Step 2. The man brings the woman down from her axis by advancing with an inside cross of his left leg. The woman responds by stepping down from her axis with an inside back opening of her left leg.

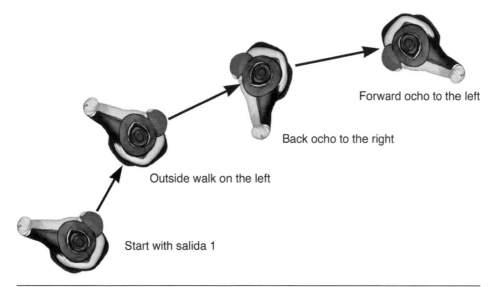

Forward ocho to the left

Back ocho to the right

Outside walk on the left

Start with salida 1

Figure 7.7 The trajectory of an alteration back right to forward left.

Step 3. The man transfers his weight completely to his left leg and marks for the woman an outside cross of her right leg. The woman responds by executing an outside cross with her right leg. The man receives the woman's outside cross by opening his right leg, placing his foot next to her right foot, and bringing her up on her axis with his embrace.

Step 4. The man holds the woman on her right axis and begins to turn to his left side, opening his left shoulder. He marks for the woman an inside forward cross by opening back with his left leg and bringing the woman gently but firmly into his left side. The woman responds by extending her left leg and advancing with an inside forward cross into the man's left side.

As a giro to the left begins with the woman's inside cross, the man may continue in a variety of ways, being aware that two steps later she will execute an outside cross with her left leg, which he could receive as the second step of la base and resolve from there. The man may receive the woman's forward step to his left as the ending of a forward ocho or as counterclockwise giro 1 or counterclockwise giro 4. This will depend on which leg he chooses to continue with—in other words, whether he stays in cross-feet position (then it is counterclockwise giro 4) or parallel (counterclockwise giro 1). But first he must turn around to change front. He can turn to the left, doing a half turn with both feet on the floor, or walk a step back with his right and turn to his left on his right axis.

Alteration Back Left to Forward Right

Watch this
demonstrated
on the DVD
This change of direction begins on an outside cross of the woman's left leg to the man's left and ends with an inside forward cross of her right leg to the man's right. The man uses diagonal openings in cross-feet system to receive the woman's crosses. Here is a common application of this change of direction (trajectory shown in figure 7.8):

Step 1. The man marks salida 1 to the woman, closes his right leg, and changes weight to enter the cross-feet system. The woman responds by assuming the salida position and holding her axis on her right leg.

Step 2. The man marks for the woman an outside cross of her left leg. The woman responds by executing an outside cross with her left. The man intersects her path, receiving her outside cross with an opening of his left leg, placing his foot next to her right foot, and bringing her up on her axis with his embrace.

Step 3. The man holds the woman on her left axis and begins to turn to his right side, opening his right shoulder. He marks for the woman an inside forward cross by opening back with his right leg and bringing the woman gently but firmly into his right side. The woman responds by extending her right leg and advancing with an inside forward cross into the man's right side.

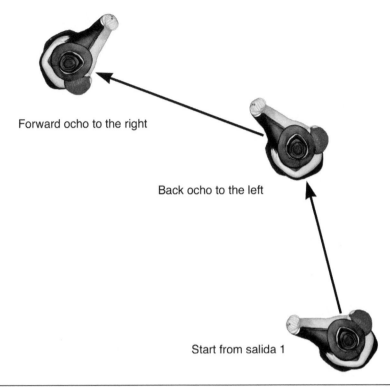

Forward ocho to the right

Back ocho to the left

Start from salida 1

Figure 7.8 The trajectory of an alteration back left to forward right.

As a giro to the right begins with the woman's inside cross, the man may continue in a variety of ways. He may receive her inside cross as the beginning of a forward ocho or as clockwise giro 1 or clockwise giro 4. This will depend on which leg he chooses to continue with—in other words, whether he stays in cross-feet position (then it is clockwise giro 4) or parallel (clockwise giro 1).

In this chapter you have learned about changing the direction of the giro, which is another way to say the direction of the woman's trajectory as she dances around the man. This is accomplished in one of two main ways. The traditional method uses similar steps of the code to end motion in one direction and start motion in the opposite direction. When the forward step is used, the resulting figure is called a forward ocho. When the back step is used, the resulting figure is called a back ocho. When an opening is used, the resulting rocking step is called an arrepentida (an evasive check, or as we have nicknamed it, "oops!").

A nontraditional, more dynamic method makes use of the fact that when the woman is dancing around the man, in between openings, one of her legs is crossed inside, or crossed outside from the perspective of the man. The change of direction is done directly from the inside to outside leg or outside to inside leg using half of a forward ocho and half of a back ocho, or vice versa, by turning the woman in the opposite direction than she normally turns for a complete ocho.

In chapter 8 continue learning how to change directions by stopping and how to alter the code of the tango.

Tangled Up? Just Tango On

No mistakes in the tango, not like life. Simple, that's what makes tango so great. You make a mistake . . . get all tangled up . . . just tango on.

—Al Pacino as "Lt. Colonel Frank Slade,"
Scent of a Woman

*T*here is a point in everybody's dancing experience where one truly begins to understand how Argentine tango dancing is about two people embraced and moving in unison around the dance floor, led by the rhythm and the melody of the music. Circulating around the floor is an acquired skill; it combines timing, balance, and improvisational skill. The man who works the conditions of the dance floor to his advantage is the one whom some female dancers generally (and mistakenly) refer to as a good "lead." That is not a compliment in Argentine tango. To the contrary, a man who "leads" may be lacking the confidence and knowledge of the dance to take on the full responsibility of managing the craft demanded by the conditions of any dance floor. He may rely on another person, generally referred to by the dehumanizing term *follow*, to guide him around the floor. A good tango dancer is a *bailarin de tango* who works the conditions of the dance floor to his advantage.

The Argentine tango dance is the intimate meeting of two people, each one fully acquainted with his or her role and fully equipped with solid technique and a deep understanding of the structure of the dance. It is not a reflection of a struggle for gender supremacy or fierce competition of one-upmanship. It is not a place for selfishness, conflicts, and mind games. It is an unspoken covenant to respect each other, work together, and contribute equally to the requirements that the dance expects from each role. One of the most important components of the man's role is to use his body and his choice of trajectories to protect his partner from injury by reckless dancing—his own and the others'. Here are some important tips for the women: The male tango dancer is not there as a pleasure and trance supplier. Having fun does not include demanding specific steps, forcing particular styles, or using him as a post to engage in self-indulgent leg flicking.

We keep emphasizing the improvisational aspects of the tango dance because it removes the shackles that learning memorized patterns places on the legs and the arms of beginning dancers. Dancing tango is about freedom to express with our bodies and our emotions the very special feelings that every tango induces in us. It takes two—as in the two of us, you and me, you and him, you and her, together as partners, with the confidence to enjoy the dance on each other's own merits, according to our level of proficiency.

In tango we trust. We trust that the man will protect his partner and dance with full understanding of the structure of the dance and the options available to him in terms of improvising for navigation. We trust that the woman will let herself be taken around the floor in an embrace that provides her motion and allows her legs to perform the important roles of supporting her balance on axis and decorating and embellishing with tasteful footwork.

TIME TO STOP AND SMELL THE ROSES

One of the most unique characteristics of the tango (beyond the fact that it is based on simple concepts for unlimited power of improvisation and the need for commitment and solid technique in equal parts by each partner) is that dancers are not required to move on every beat of the music. They can actually dance by not moving—that is, by stopping in suspended pauses. Bringing the dancing to a stop is another sophisticated way to change directions.

When the pulsating rhythm of an orchestra, the moaning of the bandoneóns, the lyrical sweetness of the violins, or the textured voice of a singer holds our bodies and souls spellbound, we could hardly be trying to remember step pattern 954B or trying to apply variation 173A that somebody showed us earlier at the local tango party. This is where the power of improvisation comes in handy. You either have it or you don't. To have it, you must have the elements and the knowledge to identify familiar body positions so that on the spur of the moment you can invent a way to move to another position without missing a beat.

As explained in chapter 6, an eight-count giro is a series of continuous turns that can be executed clockwise or counterclockwise in eight body movements. Knowing how to initiate, enter, exit, change the direction of, or stop a giro gives the dancer a powerful tool for developing creative improvisational skills. We subscribe to the belief that the whole of tango dancing is embodied in the eight-count giro. Every move we execute on the dance floor is a component of the eight-count giro. So, as a learned dancer, you should be able to identify the moves and relate to them as modified positions of the eight-count giro to create the different looks. We now introduce the concept of *paradas* (stops), *ganchos* (hooks), and *boleos* (leg flicks) as additional elements for changing directions or breaking the code of the tango.

INTRODUCTION TO THE PARADA

The term *parada* is the past participle of the Spanish verb *parar*, which literally means to stop. The name is shorthand for *la mujer ha sido parada por el hombre*, or "the woman has been stopped by the man." The definition in tango terms is the action of stopping the woman when she still has both feet on the floor (in other words, when she is transitioning between axes on

> *parada—Stop. The man stops the woman, usually as she crosses back.*

an inside or outside cross but never laterally). A man should never stop the woman while she is in the process of executing a lateral opening because it is not flattering for the woman to be seen with her legs open.

Parada With Sandwich

This popular sequence is done in the cross-feet system and occurs when the woman is executing an outside cross to the man's right (clockwise giro 6). The recognizable feature of the parada is the illusion that the man stops the woman by placing his right foot next to her left foot when she has crossed her right foot outside (see figure 8.1). You will learn that this parada is the result of interrupting the outside cross of the woman with the man's right shoulder when she has both feet on the ground. As her transition to her right axis is interrupted (that is, stopped), the woman bends her front leg and elongates her right calf, pressing against the floor with her right metatarsal and keeping the heel off the ground.

[Watch this demonstrated on the DVD]

Step 1. Set up for the parada by executing salida 1. The man closes his right leg, changing weight to enter the cross-feet system and holding the woman on her right axis. The woman responds by moving from her home position to the salida position.

Step 2. The man marks for the woman an outside cross (salida 2 or base 2) while he steps away from her, bringing his weight completely to his left axis and holding her on her left axis. He turns his upper body to his right, aligning the center of his chest with the woman's left breast.

Step 3. He opens his right arm, releasing her to bring the woman down from her left axis into his right. The woman responds by flexing her support leg and extending her right leg with an outside cross until her metatarsal makes solid contact with the floor. While holding his axis on his left leg, the man receives her outside cross by placing his right foot next to the outside edge of her left foot, matching the inner curvature of his shoe with the outer curvature of her foot. The effect is to give the illusion that the man has stopped the woman with his foot while standing on her left side (figure 8.1a).

Step 4. The man shifts the woman's weight completely to her rear leg to make room for him to stand up in front of her, sandwiching her left foot with his left foot. While standing vertically with the woman's left foot trapped in between his feet (figure 8.1b), the man changes weight to his left foot.

Step 5. The man passes over to the right side of the woman by stepping back with his right leg, crossing it outside his left leg, and bringing the woman forward to her left leg. With this simple step over, the man has changed the alignment of the bodies so that he is now on the right side of the woman (figure 8.1c). The resulting position is similar to that at the end of the cruzada position, when the woman has her weight on her left leg and is on the left side of the man, positioned to step over his left foot with an inside cross to the man's right.

Step 6. The man marks a forward step, changing his axis to his right leg and inviting the lady to step over his left foot with a slight rotation of his upper body to his right. The woman responds by turning her upper body on her left hip to face the right shoulder of the man. She steps forward toward the right side of the man with an inside front cross of her right leg.

Step 7. The man receives the beginning of her forward ocho, bringing her up on her right axis and turning her body to position it for the completion of the forward ocho. The woman responds by finishing her forward step, holding her axis, and allowing her body to turn to change direction.

Step 8. The man marks for the woman an inside forward cross with her left leg by shifting his weight to his left leg. The woman responds by stepping forward toward the left side of the man with an inside forward cross of her left leg. The man brings his right leg to a close, changing weight and turning the lady on her left axis to face him. The woman responds by finishing the forward step, holding her axis, and assuming the cruzada position.

Figure 8.1 The parada with sandwich can be executed any time the woman is doing an outside cross of her right leg.

Resolving from the cruzada position should be obvious by now. The parada with sandwich can be executed anytime the woman is doing an outside cross of her right leg. Technically, it originates on the sixth position of the eight-count giro to the right (clockwise giro 6) when the man, in cross-feet system, stops the woman as she crosses her right leg outside and extends his right foot, placing it next to her left foot.

Notice that by stopping the woman on an outside cross when he is on her left side and passing over to her right side, the man converts the woman's position to the forward opening that precedes her inside forward cross. Rather than change the direction of the giro, when she advances again she still is in right-hand giro mode, she starts her change of front again with an inside forward cross.

Using solid knowledge to modify set patterns, altering a movement, making a decision on the spot, and continuing to dance with flair, fluidity, grace, elegance, and poise are the most obvious results of having a talent for improvisation. Improvisation is what leads to fancy dancing on a crowded floor.

There is a similar parada with a sandwich on the sixth position of the eight-count giro to the left (counterclockwise giro 6). In this case, the man stops the woman when she is on an outside cross of her left leg toward the left side of the man.

Step 1. With weight on his right leg, the man stops the woman as she crosses her left leg outside. The woman responds the same way as explained previously: forward knee slightly bent, back metatarsal firmly planted, back heel off the floor.

Step 2. The man places his left foot on the outside of her right foot, matching the inner curvature of his shoe with the outer curvature of her foot.

Step 3. The man shifts the woman's weight to her rear leg by transferring his full weight to his left leg and sandwiching her right foot between his left and right foot. Then, while standing vertically with the woman's left foot trapped in between his feet, the man changes weight to his right foot and passes over to her left, sidestepping back with a back cross of his left leg.

Step 4. The man brings the lady to her forward axis on her right leg and invites her to step over his right foot with an inside forward cross of her left leg to his left. This is similar to the end of a forward ocho, so the man resolves with a resolution.

The use of the parada must be handled with the rest of the dancers in mind. Stopping for no other reason than to do a parada just because you learned how to do it may create circulation problems for the other couples coming from behind you. It is accepted dance floor etiquette to drop toward the center of the dance floor before engaging in any figure that may otherwise block the flow of traffic on the edges of the dance floor. After you play and have fun, rejoin the line of dance anywhere that doesn't interfere with the flow.

INTRODUCTION TO THE GANCHO

Another way to interrupt the motion of the woman for the purpose of changing her direction is the leg hook, commonly known as *gancho*. The position where the gancho takes place is the same sixth position of the eight-count giro (clockwise giro 6 and counterclockwise giro 6); in other words, it is when the woman steps back with her outside leg using a cross behind her support leg. In this case, the man interrupts and stops the woman's motion by extending his outside leg to block the thigh of her inside leg. Next, he changes her axis to the outside leg with a *gentle* forward lunge into her, flexing his support knee. Then he marks a backward motion of her inside leg. Since the man is blocking that leg at the thigh, the woman can move only her inside leg until her thigh presses firmly against the man's thigh. She continues moving her leg from the knee down, wrapping the upper part of her leg on the man's thigh, thus hooking her leg into the man's open stance (see figure 8.2).

> *gancho—Hook. A compound move that interrupts the woman's back step with a block by the man's body and his leg, which is then bent to provide a place for the intended energy to go. It ends with her embellished blocked back step, the gancho, before being converted to a forward step.*

Four-Step Gancho Sequence to the Left

Watch this demonstrated on the DVD

Step 1. Begin from the home position with the first step of the salida, salida 1. The man closes his right foot and changes weight while holding the woman on her right axis.

Step 2. With his weight on his right axis, the man turns the woman to his left, marking an outside cross of her left leg. The woman responds by stepping back with her left leg. As soon as her left leg makes contact with the floor, the man extends his left leg and places his left foot next to her left foot, blocking her right thigh.

Step 3. The man flexes his left knee to bring his weight over that leg and brings the woman gently to her left axis. The man elongates his upper body so that the woman stands on her left axis with a straight knee. Then he turns her hips slightly to her left, allowing her right leg to move back into him, first making full thigh-to-thigh contact and then wrapping the upper part of her leg into his thigh.

Step 4. The man changes his axis back to his right leg. He straightens his left leg. He brings the woman down from her left axis back to her right axis. The woman responds by returning her right foot in an inside forward cross to the same place it was before the initiation of the gancho.

The real purpose of a leg hook is to change the direction of the woman from a counterclockwise trajectory into the man's left to a clockwise direction to the man's right. In other words, the counterclockwise giro has changed to a clockwise giro. The movement resolves with a forward ocho and resolution, although it can connect to a clockwise giro.

The return of the gancho to the left may be seen as a clockwise giro 4, the fourth step of the eight-count giro. The man can turn to his right and make the woman walk a second forward step, this time with her outside leg. Since the man is not moving from his axis position, the woman responds by allowing her upper body to turn on her right axis and opening her left leg laterally around the man, which is the equivalent of clockwise giro 5, the fifth

Figure 8.2 A properly executed leg hook, or gancho.

step of the eight-count giro. The man receives her opening with a closing of his left foot and a change of weight. The setup allows the execution of another hook to the right.

Step 1. With his weight on his left axis, the man turns the lady to his right, marking an outside cross of her right leg behind her left axis. The lady responds by stepping back with her right leg. As soon as the lady's right leg goes down to the floor, the man extends his right leg to step right next to her right foot at an angle, such that his extended right leg makes contact with the lady's support leg (he blocks her left thigh).

Step 2. The man lunges forward, bending his right knee to bring his weight over that leg. He places the lady's axis completely on her right leg. At the same time, the man elongates his upper body so that the woman stands on her right axis. Then he turns her hips slightly to her right, making room for her left leg to come back into him, first making full contact thigh to thigh, and then wrapping the upper part of her leg around his thigh.

Step 3. Finally the man changes his axis back to his left leg, straightening his right leg and bringing the lady down from her right axis forward into her left axis. The lady responds by returning her left foot to the position it was in before the hook.

Once again the direction of the lady has changed through the execution of a leg hook. We can consider a couple of repetitions of left-leg hook, right-leg hook for effect, but only if the action does not interfere with the flow of traffic. From either side of the leg hook, the change of direction positions the woman to start with a forward cross of her inside leg. Use a forward ocho and resolution to end, or pick up the eight-count giro in the new direction.

INTRODUCTION TO THE BOLEO

We now introduce the concept of breaking the code of the tango. Indeed, rules were made to be broken. Rules can be broken after you have a thorough understanding of their purpose. So in breaking the rules, you can also do so with a purpose. A boleo is one figure that you can use to break or alter the code of the tango.

The code of tango specifies that as the woman dances around the man, she alternates the crossing of the trailing leg on the outside and inside.

boleo—The action of interrupting an outside cross, converting it to an inside cross, or vice versa.

That means that when she dances around the man's left, the woman leads (opens) with her right leg and crosses her left leg. When she dances around the man's right, the woman leads (opens) with her left leg and crosses her right leg.

The main purpose of the boleo is to alter the natural progression of the code by replacing the expected crossing of a leg with the opposite crossing. The result is that the motion continues in the same direction with a repetition of the last cross, creating a different look (see figure 8.3, on page 150). The two forms of boleo available to each leg are a back boleo and a front boleo.

To state it in accordance with our use of the eight-count giro as the source of all the tango moves, back boleos are interruptions of the third and sixth positions of the eight-count giro, converted to the first and fourth positions of the eight-count giro, respectively. For example, as an eight-count giro reaches its third position (clockwise giro 3 or counterclockwise giro 3), it is expected that the woman will cross her outside leg behind to step back into the direction that she is moving. If the outside cross is interrupted halfway through its motion by holding the lady on her inside axis, the outside leg will go around in a circular trajectory until it reaches the full extension allowed by the rotation of the hips. Then it will rebound, retracing the circular pattern, and come around the support axis to cross inside front and continue the trajectory without changing the front (that is, it will repeat the first step of the eight-count giro).

Similarly, as the eight-count giro reaches its fourth position, it is expected that the lady will cross her inside leg in front to step forward into the direction that she is moving. If the forward step is interrupted halfway through its motion by holding the lady on her outside axis, the inside leg will wrap around the support leg in a circular way until it reaches the full extension allowed by the rotation of the hips. Then it will rebound, retracing the circular pattern, and come around the support axis to cross outside behind the support leg and continue the trajectory, either in the third or the sixth position of the eight-count giro, depending on whether the man receives her motion in parallel or cross-feet system.

What catches people's eyes and creates the illusion of a flying leg arcing its way around the support leg is the woman embellishing the move by raising her foot off the floor when the motion of her leg is interrupted and begins to return, and then letting the foot drop when the leg passes next to the support leg. Such a simple task eludes many women who prefer to imitate what they see (most of the time an illusion, a sleight of legs) rather than to internalize and understand the dynamics of partner dancing. When acting on the illusion, they hold on to their partners for dear life in order to swing the free leg, which is incorrect.

Back boleos may be initiated from the lateral opening that precedes a back crossing of the outside leg or from the back crossing that precedes a traditional change of direction using back ochos. The main difference between a boleo originating from an opening and a boleo originating from a back step on a change of direction is that there is no pivot of the support leg on the boleo from the lateral opening. The leg chosen for the boleo comes directly in contact with the support leg. The knee presses firmly behind the support knee and bends to send the lower part of the leg around the support axis. The support hip does all the work of the boleo; the action of the hip changing direction produces the movement of the free nonsupport leg.

As you continue to use your knowledge and resources, you can identify familiar positions from which to execute a boleo: the first step of the salida, the second step of the resolution, and every time the woman is positioned to cross inside or outside.

Back Boleo and Then Front Boleo

Step 1. Begin from a salida. The dancers move laterally toward the left side of the man. The man marks a side step of the woman's right leg, opening laterally with his left leg *and* closing his right leg halfway to form a triangle with his left foot and the woman's open feet. Watch this demonstrated on the DVD

Step 2. Holding her firmly on her right axis with a tight embrace, the man does a quick change of weight to his right axis and quickly rotates his upper body to his left enough to produce lateral pressure with his right arm on the woman's left side. She responds by allowing her support hip to absorb the lateral pressure with a turn of the outer hip, which brings the open left leg to a close. The woman flexes her right axis and places her left knee slightly behind her support knee to keep her thighs closed. The woman then allows her lower leg to continue tracing a circle around and behind her support leg, flexing her left knee and keeping her right foot on the floor.

Step 3. The man quickly changes his axis back to his left leg as soon as the woman's left foot extends fully behind the support leg. This upper-body countermotion forces the woman's left leg to bounce back from behind, retracing a circle and coming around the support leg. The woman responds by allowing the free leg to be pulled back by the upper-body counterrotation. She has the option of embellishing the return of the leg being flicked by raising her foot and letting it drop by virtue of gravity. This is the illusion that observers notice: a flying foot on an elliptical trajectory.

Step 4. The man holds the woman on her right axis long enough for her thighs to close when the left leg finishes its return and marks an inside forward cross into his left. The woman responds by stepping forward with her inside (left) leg into the same spot she would have stepped with the interrupted back step.

Step 5. The man receives the woman's forward step, closing his right leg and shifting weight. The woman responds by turning to face the man, crossing her right foot behind her left axis, and assuming the cruzada position.

Step 6. The man advances with his left leg while the woman responds by opening to his left with her right leg and begins a resolution to end the sequence.

Figure 8.3 Proper leg embellishment for back and front boleo.

The key ingredient in executing a correct boleo is the position of the man's foot in relation to the woman's feet. The idea for the man is to step as close as possible to the center of the woman's opening so that her axis is in the center of his body. An opportunity for a boleo may be found on a right-hand eight-count giro. For that, combine a simple salida with the fourth position of the eight-count giro (clockwise giro 4).

Step 1. Start with a simple salida. At salida 4 the man holds his right leg without changing weight. Thus they enter the cross-feet system.

Step 2. With his weight on his left axis, the man marks the woman an inside forward cross. She responds by advancing with an inside forward cross of her right leg. The man begins to turn to his right and extends his right leg toward the lady's right shoulder, crossing the line of her feet and placing his right foot in front of her left foot. This is the fourth position of the eight-count giro (clockwise giro 4).

Step 3. Still turning to his right, the man transfers his weight to his right leg, making the woman's upper body turn on her right axis. The woman responds by completing her forward step, placing her left leg next to her right leg without weight. As the man completes his weight transfer to his right leg and makes a new axis, the rotation of his upper body makes the woman "fall" off her axis. The woman responds with a lateral opening, allowing her left leg to move forward and around into the space behind the man. As the woman's left foot lands toward the man's right side, the man opens his left leg forward. He extends it crossing the line of the feet, placing his foot right in the center of her open legs to form a triangle with his foot and the woman's feet.

Step 4. The man continues rotating to his right, advances forward by transferring his weight to his left leg, and sends the woman's right leg around behind her support leg while holding her vertical on her left axis and not allowing her to shift her axis to her right leg. The woman responds by holding her axis firmly over her left leg, allowing her support hip to rotate, bringing her right knee behind the left knee, and bending her left knee so the lower part of the leg continues to go around behind in a circle.

Step 5. As the woman's right leg reaches full extension behind the support leg, the man quickly brings his right foot to his left foot and changes weight, turning slightly to his left. The woman responds by allowing her upper body to begin turning to her left while her hips are still turning to her right. This produces a ricochet effect as the lower right leg finally stops and begins to be pulled back by the pressure of the upper body over the support hip. The woman may embellish the return of the right foot by picking it up as soon as the return trajectory begins and letting it drop on its own on the half beat.

Step 6. When the woman's right leg comes together with the support (left) leg, the man steps back with his left leg, bringing the woman down from her axis with a forward step to his right. The woman responds by extending her right leg down and into the right side of the man. This position is identical to base 5, so the man resolves by finishing la base on his right axis and holding the woman on her left axis. Alternatively, after the woman's forward step with her right leg, the man may treat her step as the beginning of a forward ocho and finish it with a resolution.

A boleo is a natural consequence of modifying the sequence in which a turn progresses. Remember that lateral openings, inside crosses, and outside crosses are the elements of the code of the tango and the way the woman dances by surrounding the man to his right or left. Boleos are another way to alter the predictable sequences of turns and provide additional options for navigation. They are not designer figures executed without any context to the dance. In other words, we encourage dancers not to stage figures like boleos by stopping in the middle of the floor and interfering with the flow and safety of other dancers. When dancing on a crowded floor, the woman should choose not to do the embellished boleo; rather, she should let her free foot remain on the floor, drawing the shape of the arc it is taking. The best way to get comfortable with boleos during a turn is to understand where the boleo can take place in the process of turning. During a turn the man uses clockwise giro 5, position 5 of the eight-count giro, to mark a boleo.

Another position where a back boleo may be applied is during a change of direction using the third step (outside cross) of the code. Anytime the woman moves to either side of the man with an outside cross, a change of direction resolves in an identical outside cross to the opposite direction. A back boleo in this instance will eliminate the outside cross and begin with the woman moving in the new direction with an inside forward cross. As an example of unlimited options available to the dancers, here is a variation of the salida that has two changes of direction built in to arrive at the same cruzada position (fourth step of the regular salida). It offers a prime opportunity to use the back boleo.

Step 1. From the home position, the man starts with a short lateral step to his left, making the woman step long to his left so that he is on her left side. The man holds the woman on her right axis and quickly closes his right foot, changing weight to enter the cross-feet system.

Step 2. With the woman on his left, the man marks a back step of the woman's left leg and advances with a forward step of his left leg, using the same lane where her left leg is.

Step 3. The man transfers his weight onto his left leg and opens forward with his right leg, marking an outside cross of her right leg. The woman responds by crossing her outside right leg behind her left leg and stepping back.

Step 4. The man transfers his weight completely to his right leg, forming a triangle with the woman's crossed legs, and initiates a change of her direction by shifting her axis completely to her back (right) leg and making her pivot on it to her left.

Step 5. As she pivots, the woman's left leg closes next to her right and now becomes her outside leg, crossing behind the support (right) leg with an extension into the man's left, beginning a back ocho.

Step 6. As soon as the woman's left leg extends behind her support leg, the man holds the woman on her right axis, not allowing her to change axis to her left with a step. He quickly shifts his axis to his left to turn her upper body in the opposite direction. The woman responds by allowing the opposite turn of her upper body to stop the rotation of her hip with a snapping motion. This brings her left leg around from behind in a circular forward motion that continues into a forward step to the same spot where the interrupted back step would have landed.

Step 7. As the woman steps forward with her left leg, the man closes his right leg, shifting weight so that the woman continues her motion surrounding the man to his left.

Step 8. The man advances with his left leg while the woman is opening to his left with her right leg, and he begins a resolution to end the sequence.

A front boleo is a more difficult and therefore less popular movement that is executed mostly by stage dancers or those who understand the mechanics of the boleo and its purpose. We expect you to be among those who are capable of using the front boleo as another tool to enhance your navigational skills.

As you'll see, a front boleo is an interruption of an inside forward cross that is replaced by an outside cross. What better opportunity for a front boleo than the return from a back boleo? Indeed, you should now be familiar with the back boleo. As soon as the woman's leg comes around her support leg, positioned to step forward with an inside forward cross, the man changes axis back in the opposite direction to force her upper body to turn in the opposite direction her hips are moving. The delayed effect snaps the hip and brings the leg back around the support leg to cross behind in a circular motion, resuming the direction change with the original back step. In other words, the man interrupts the back step with a back boleo, which brings the free leg around to step forward. Immediately he interrupts the forward step with a front boleo, which sends the leg behind to continue with the original intended back step.

In a conceptual form, the boleo is the result of a countermotion of the man around the woman, which interrupts a back or forward step and converts it into a forward or back step, respectively. In the time frame of one step, the man marks the beginning of a step (say a back step). While the woman's leg is traveling back, the man walks in double time around the woman in the opposite direction to force the counterturn of the woman's upper body to bring the leg back from behind and pass it in front of the support leg. Remember that the flying-foot effect is an embellishment that the woman executes by lifting and letting her foot drop on its own. Similarly, if the woman's inside leg is coming forward (whether from a back boleo or a forward ocho) while her leg is traveling forward, the man may walk in double time around the woman in the opposite direction to force the counterturn of her upper body to bring the leg back from the front and pass it behind the support leg.

In summary, you have learned about paradas, ganchos, and boleos as additional tools to change directions or front. You use a parada to stop the woman from turning in to one direction. When the man passes over to her other side, he changes the center of her rotating trajectory in the same direction.

You use ganchos (leg hooks) to stop the progression of a turn and change the direction of the turn without the use of pivots or alterations. A gancho is another way to interrupt the motion of the woman for the purposes of changing her direction in a giro. A left-hand eight-count giro ends on the back step being blocked by the gancho and continues to the right on a forward step. A right-hand eight-count giro ends on the back step being blocked by the gancho and continues to the left on a forward step.

Finally, the boleo is perhaps one of the most spectacular moves because of the dramatic effect that the woman may add by lifting the foot off the floor and letting it drop on its own while the leg is going around the support axis. Its main purpose is to alter the sequence of the code as the woman goes through a change of front surrounding the man.

The cupboard is just about equipped with all the major ingredients that any dancers desiring to become masters of improvisation would want to have available in order to start cooking up some exhilarating figures for the delight of their partners. We promise you that your patience, dedication, and hard work will lead to hours of enjoyment in tango dancing.

Doing Argentine Tango on Your Own

CHAPTER 9

Fancy Dancing
on a Crowded Floor

Etiquette must, if it is to be of more than trifling use, include ethics as well as manners.

—*Emily Post*

You have done all the lessons. You understand your role. You have mastered your own balance and axis. You understand why you dance and how to dance Argentine tango. You have your favorite music playing in your head. You have your new dance shoes. You feel the need to express yourself by using the tools you have to create a myriad of your own figures. You are a tango dancer!

So you need to find a place to dance. Argentine tango is not the popular dance filling up the nightclubs and discos worldwide, so an almost underground effort exists to provide places for you to use all those lessons to complete your journey of becoming a social dancer. In the jargon of the Argentine tango, what we call a tango dance party, or the place where we go to dance, is a *milonga* in Buenos Aires. Although it would be impossible to replicate the environment, the social interaction, and the accepted codes of the milongas of Buenos Aires outside their habitat, most larger cities have their tango dance parties and call them, euphemistically, *milongas*; smaller cities might have one each week or each month. There might be something called a *práctica*, or a practice session.

A typical large city milonga.

FINDING MILONGAS

The milonga, whether on a weeknight or on a weekend, is *the* place to dance tango. In the United States, it might be held in a dance studio, or perhaps a bar or a restaurant willing to give up moneymaking space for a tango night. It can be plain or fancy, depending on the host or organizer. Most organizers try to create a nightclub atmosphere with some or all of the elements including low lighting, candles, little tables, and adult drinks. There is an attempt to provide a social atmosphere. Dancers tend to dress up, but not in costume. They call it *elegant sport* in Buenos Aires. Perhaps things are a bit more sporty (trousers for the ladies, no jackets for the gentlemen) on the weeknight and more festive on weekends.

In larger cities, weekend milongas tend to start later in the evening, usually around 10 p.m., and go until 2 or 3 a.m. On a weeknight a milonga might begin at as early as 7 p.m. and end as early as 10 p.m. or go until midnight or 1 a.m. Sometimes a class is given an hour before the social dancing starts. This is a good way to meet other dancers you can dance with socially later in the evening. Every city has its own hours of operation, depending on the social habits of that particular place. In some cities teachers or organizers hold tango nights in commercial places with regular hours of operation. If it's a restaurant, dinner hours will be the hours of tango time. If it's a bar, the hours might be later.

The práctica might be an event in itself, or it might take place after a formal class. It is usually held in a more basic environment: a dance studio, a school hall, or a church basement. It starts earlier in the evening. The lights

are full up. The dress is casual as
for a dance class. Refreshments are
not typically served, although every
organizer is different. Usually people

*práctica—An informal practice
session for tango dancers.*

just dance with each other. If a teacher is present, he or she will be available
for questions and guidance. Dancers also share steps, problems, and discoveries with each other. We could say that the difference between a práctica
and a milonga, in terms of protocol, is that at a práctica, talking, teaching,
and coaching on the dance floor are perfectly acceptable behaviors as long
as they are consensual.

When you want to find a place to dance, ask your teachers, fellow students,
and other dancers. Sometimes a venue might be listed in a local newspaper.
There is a tremendous amount of information on the Internet. (A comprehensive list of links to tango Web sites around the world maybe found at
www.planet-tango.com/tangolin.htm.) Call or e-mail the organizers ahead
of time to make sure there are no changes in schedule. There is nothing more
disappointing than to show up with your heart set on dancing only to find
the place is closed for the night.

What's a Milonga?

In the last week of 2004, a major fire engulfed an overcrowded Buenos Aires
club during the climax of a rock concert. Hundreds of young people perished in
what turned out to be a firetrap of major proportions. Soon it became evident
that corruption and graft had allowed the establishment to circumvent fire
inspections and operate without the proper fire safeguards. Almost immediately, the city government shut down every dance hall in the city, enforcing a
draconian set of regulations that required inspections, installation of clearly
marked emergency exits, and a set capacity limit according to the size of each
place. The milongas of Buenos Aires were severely affected by the blanket
ordinance, and for many weeks they were not allowed to operate.

The Association of Organizers of Milongas (AOM) went to work immediately
to assist the many milonga organizers who simply had been renting space at
social clubs and ethnic associations for their weekly milongas. A great lobbying effort was orchestrated to persuade the cultural secretary of the City of
Buenos Aires to issue a special dispensation to exempt the milongas from the
decree closing all dance halls until further notice. To support their request and
prove their point, the AOM cited a law that had declared tango a national
patrimony of cultural interest and submitted the following definition of a
milonga as part of their success in obtaining the special dispensation that
allowed the milongas to reopen within weeks.

1. A milonga is a place where the dance of tango and its codes of conduct
   are taught and practiced. It is also the social encounter that is generated later when a dance is organized.

2. In a milonga the dance floor is clearly demarcated from and surrounded by the area occupied by tables and chairs where the public remain seated, except when they step onto the dance floor to dance.

3. The structure of this type of dance requires sufficient space for its execution as well as the additional space for the circulation around, which is also preordained by this dance. That determines its capacity. The number of tables and chairs needed to accommodate everyone in attendance and the need for circulation corridors for the waiters to take care of servicing the tables result in an especially low density of participants in relation to the other dance halls, where agglomeration is the norm.

4. The public is mainly adult, with a certain level of education. They are local *habitués* and foreigners who come to practice or to perfect the knowledge of the dance.

5. The atmosphere is familiar, similar to a social club, where the majority of people know each other. There are particularly demanding codes of conduct and courtesy, which are as important as the knowledge of the dance itself.

6. The lighting, unlike in the dance halls, must be relatively high to allow all the participants to get a good look at all the premises. A minimum of approximately 40 lux is required.

7. The music must have a low decibel level in order to avoid affecting the auditory capacity of the public engaged in normal conversations at the tables. (Normal is considered approximately 75 decibels; 130 decibels is the level at a disco, which is barely bearable for less than 15 minutes without causing a reduction in the level of hearing.)

8. The dance is done exclusively in pairs.

9. The presence of live music does not modify any of these parameters. The patrons remain seated at the tables or dance on the floor with conduct identical to that acceptable for recorded music. In other instances, when a singer performs or professional dancers give a dance exhibition, the duration does not exceed the length of a tanda and the patrons remain seated, without crowding any areas or exceeding capacity of a space.

10. All these conditions (lighting, sound level, characteristics of the music, quality of the dance, codes of courtesy, and age of the patrons) contribute to an atmosphere of intimacy at the milonga that is conducive to calm and friendly behavior, diametrically opposed to what is characteristic of other places of dance.

Minding Your Manners

Since you are an adult dancing tango, simply apply your own social skills to the social aspects at the tango venue. Lacking social skills is a major handicap that only you can overcome. First acknowledge what you lack in social manners, and then work to acquire them.

When you arrive, greet your host. Find a place to sit down and check out the room, but please do not change your shoes at your table (or the place you are sitting). It is customary to change your shoes in the restroom or the coatroom. Good hosts provide a chair or two away from the dance floor to do the personal task of changing from street shoes to dance shoes.

In some cities, there is a minimum of conversation. In other cities, people chat each other up before segueing into a night's worth of dancing. If you are new, just settle in for a few minutes and observe what everyone is doing. If you have a problem (you don't like the music, it's too hot or too cold, the refreshments are gone, the floor is too sticky, the floor is too slippery), direct it to the organizer, but don't be a spoiler. Be nice or leave.

There is a saying in New Orleans: "If you liked it, tell all your friends; if you didn't like it, don't tell nobody." The people who organize milongas and prácticas deserve support and respect, particularly when they invest the money and the time required to plan and produce a great evening for all. Some have full-time jobs and organize social opportunities as a second job and do so for either love or very little money. Professionals who make their living teaching tango also give classes and organize milongas for love and money. It is an effort, sometimes a huge effort that benefits all who want to go out and dance Argentine tango.

The codes of the milongas in the United States are loose, and they vary from location to location and from organizer to organizer. Time-honored Argentine traditions may seem tedious, outdated, and foreign to those eager to go out and just have fun, and that is quite understandable. A *tango dance party* is a more descriptive term to describe what is done outside Buenos Aires. Being able to understand the difference between a milonga and a dance party gives us a good reality check and keeps us honest with ourselves. At tango dance parties in the United States, cigarette smoke is nonexistent, hard liquor is seldom poured, and above all, the formality with which the rituals of the Buenos Aires milongas are conducted is almost nonexistent.

PAIRING UP

In Buenos Aires the couple is respected and honored as the ultimate configuration of dancing tango. As a couple, you are expected to dance with each other. Instead of being perceived as a second choice, it is thought of as the ultimate choice. Dancing with your *pareja*, as a significant other is called in Buenos Aires, is exciting and romantic. It is an accomplishment you will both always remember and want to do again.

There are often more female dancers than male dancers, so the question arises regarding the appropriateness of the lady asking for a dance. There are no rules. Well, actually, there are a few: Be polite, behave in a friendly manner, and do not demand a dance or recriminate the lack of one. Do what is comfortable and socially correct. Women, be feminine. You are role-playing the maximum feminine part when you choose to dance Argentine tango. Don't ask men by saying, "You owe me a dance." It would be nicer to say, "This is a great tango; could we try it?" "I'd love to dance with you" is a flattery almost impossible to resist. Accept that he might decline your request, and take it with good nature. When a dancer declines, it is seldom personal. Sometimes it's because of fatigue or a bad mood or dislike for the particular tango being played.

How women present themselves has much to do with how much they dance. However, collecting dances, or monopolizing the pool of male dancers, is not an indicator of skill or a measure of how good a time you had that night. If you think you need a certain number of dances to validate your experience, you will always be disappointed. Of course, we come to the dance party to dance. But sometimes it doesn't go that way. Adopting an attitude of being content enough to enjoy an evening out, no matter how many dances you get, will serve you well. You must be optimistic. If it wasn't your night, you'll live to dance another night.

In Buenos Aires, the codes of the milongas are a whole different game. Women and men who come to dance keep their conversation to a minimum. However, in between dances, whether by their own decision or perhaps by not being able to connect to a potential partner, people have a drink and a bite to eat and catch up on the latest gossip with their table companions. They also listen to the music, watch the floor show of their fellow dancers, and then go home and dream a tango. In the United States people chat to socialize. If a milonga feels "militant," with expressed or implied rules, well, then, it's just no fun. Just use common sense. Chat, but dance too, be nice, and go home and dream a tango. Emily Post notes, "Good manners in clubs are the same as good manners elsewhere, only a little more so."

Same-gender dancing was a huge issue in the mid-1990s. Argentine tango is thought to be the traditional role-playing between a man and a woman. Times change. The idea of who and what define a couple has changed. If the tango is respected and danced in a considerate manner by any couple, there is room for everyone on the dance floor. If a woman is assuming the man's role, she should be able to navigate with skill. There is nothing more awful than two women acting silly, not knowing what they are doing, banging into people, and expecting to be tolerated because they are just having fun. If two men want to dance together, they should mind their space and not let it become an athletic display that disturbs the space of other dancers. If you are not comfortable accepting an offer to dance with someone of your gender, decline politely. If you are turned down, accept it with grace. No one should be made to feel defensive in a social situation. Above all, no matter on which side of the equation you choose to be, dance the tango with respect for its traditions and with consideration for others on the same dance floor. Avoid being an embarrassment to the hosts, to your fellow dancers, to yourself, and to the dance itself.

Guidelines for Being a DJ at a Milonga

The milonga is not the place to force music on people that they otherwise may not want to hear. A music appreciation night somewhere else and at another time would be a more appropriate way to explore personal taste.

The milonga is not the place for electronic music—tango or otherwise.

The music at a milonga must be of the variety of tango styles so that people who know how to dance can dance, and those who don't can learn.

The milonga is the ultimate tango education for regulars and newcomers.

By accepting the role of DJ, you run the risk that some may leave because of your choice to play tango, or perhaps not come at all when you work, but that is better than people leaving or not showing up when you work as a DJ because you don't play tango.

In the beginning it is a good idea to use proven and successful methods. Purchase or borrow compilations of "made-by-DJs-for-milonga" CDs. Learn the sequences, the changes in mood, and the chemistry within a tanda.

After years of learning from what successful DJs have been doing in Buenos Aires to pack the most popular milongas, we have become very experienced DJs and always carry with us 18 unique CDs (compilations of tangos, valses, and milongas) that can last for six weeks of weekly DJing without repeating a single song. Our expertise allows us also to mix them randomly, providing an infinite number of nonrepetitive tandas that will keep the die-hards on the floor until the end of the night begging for more when it is time to go home.

One thing we never do is to impose personal taste. Rather, we learn what a good dancer would need and appreciate to have a good dance. Then, we try hard to play music for them.

Newer dancers are schooled by hearing the top 300 standards over and over, getting into a comfort zone that allows them to dance alongside and with seasoned veterans. Experienced dancers depend on the standard 300 as the tried-and-true formula for a good night of dancing tango.

Humility is the mother of all virtues. During the development period of a dance community, the DJ should simply be a designated Play button pusher every week. He or she has the responsibilities of selecting the CDs to use and then pushing the Play button again after the first CD ends.

When a gentleman asks a woman to dance, he should note where he picked her up and return her to that place at the end of their time together. It is an accomplishment by design or coincidence if you can do this by ending your tango together at that place where you started dancing. If this does not happen, then the gentleman should walk the lady back to her table or to wherever she was when she accepted the dance. It is abrupt for either partner to leave the other one standing alone on the dance floor after the tango is finished. It is downright rude to do it in order to rush away and intercept another dancer escorting or being escorted back. Gentlemen, if a lady declines a dance for any reason, accept it without defensive feelings. Ladies who choose to decline a dance should do so with kindness and a simple "no, thank you."

DANCING SETS

Customs vary so much as to how long that time together on the dance floor might be. In Buenos Aires it's usual to dance an entire set of tangos (called *tandas*) together. The tangos are organized in sets of three or four similar tangos, milongas, or valses. This allows you to dance favorite music with favorite partners. Also, tangos are relatively short pieces of music, usually three minutes long on average. Dancing a set allows the couple to settle into a groove. The first tango is a gentle exploration. How does he or she feel? Are there axis and balance? Can he mark a simple movement? Can she respond? The second is the time to explore a little more. Can he execute a turn? Can she? The third is usually a complete understanding for the two. The fourth is the icing on the cake before the couple departs for the moment.

In social dance situations in the United States, dancing one dance is considered polite. We encourage you to dance at least two tangos. Some milongas held in the States have adopted the style of playing tandas, so if you are up to it, by all means dance the set. We advise the gentlemen to go easy on the first tango. Feel out where the woman is. If she is less experienced, do not put expert demands on her. As you embark on the next tango, you can try to do a little more (just dance in your *mutual* comfort zone).

If a man and woman spend the whole night dancing together, it could be assumed that they are keeping company. Some couples (married or otherwise) prefer to dance only with each other. Social dancing in North America tends to be an all-inclusive experience. Everybody changes partners often to enjoy dancing with friends. If you have problems with this, it is best to resolve them before you go out dancing.

1. Tango: El flete, Juan D'Arienzo
2. Tango: Rawson, Juan D'Arienzo
3. Tango: Retintin, Juan D'Arienzo
4. Tango: El cencerro, Juan D'Arienzo

Cortina (short—up to 30 seconds—musical separator, something different from tango, milonga, or vals)

5. Milonga: Reliquias porteñas, Francisco Canaro
6. Milonga: No hay tierra como la mia, Francisco Canaro
7. Milonga: La milonga de Buenos Aires, Francisco Canaro

Cortina

8. Tango: Derecho viejo, Osvaldo Pugliese
9. Tango: La rayuela, Osvaldo Pugliese
10. Tango: Mala junta, Osvaldo Pugliese
11. Tango: Recuerdo, Osvaldo Pugliese

Cortina

12. Tango: Cachirulo, Anibal Troilo
13. Tango: Guapeando, Anibal Troilo
14. Tango: Cordon de oro, Anibal Troilo
15. Tango: Toda mi vida, Anibal Troilo

Cortina

16. Vals: Soñar y nada mas, Alfredo De Angelis
17. Vals: Flores del alma, Alfredo De Angelis
18. Vals: Pobre flor, Alfredo De Angelis

Cortina

19. Tango: A la gran muñeca, Carlos Di Sarli
20. Tango: Don Juan, Carlos Di Sarli
21. Tango: El ingeniero, Carlos Di Sarli
22. Tango: Comme il faut, Carlos Di Sarli

Cortina

23. Tango: Muchachos comienza la ronda, Ricardo Tanturi
24. Tango: Oigo tu voz, Ricardo Tanturi
25. Tango: Una noche de garufa, Ricardo Tanturi
26. Tango: Comparsa criolla, Ricardo Tanturi

Cortina

27. Vals: Mendocina, Pedro Laurenz
28. Vals: Paisaje, Pedro Laurenz
29. Vals: Mascarita, Pedro Laurenz

FOCUSING ON DETAILS

If you are a new dancer, concentrate on what you know. Gentlemen, hold the woman well. Make your weight changes. Use your right arm and shoulder to indicate her movement. Dance in diagonals, bringing her to your left or right side or moving into her right or left side. Break up your movements in building blocks. The salida is one building block moving to your left. The resolution is another building block to your right. Back and forward ochos are direction changes that can be used for embellishing the salida. Giros are used for navigation to your right or left. Think about your foot placement. Keep your shoulders relaxed. Soften your knees. Of course, both of you are listening to the music and responding to it. The music, your partner, and the conditions of the floor will all dictate how the dance is navigated and improvised. Ladies, hold your axis, respond to movement (or lack of it), and let yourself be moved. Mind your foot placement and your focus, listen to the music, and stay relaxed.

As you can see, there are so many details to distract you from the joy of just dancing. It is overwhelming at first. The man might be nervous about navigation. He might be afraid to knock her into someone. He might be worried that he will not know enough to not be boring. He wants to dance his partner well. The woman worries that she might not understand the mark. She worries that he might try to trick her into making a mistake. She does not want to be boring. She wants to give her partner a good dance. All this is normal. It is something every new dancer must experience. The beauty of the thing is that it does not take too long to find a comfort zone that enables you to dance. As you put in the hours, things get easier, and your dancing evolves. The more you dance socially, the faster your progress. The more you work together as equals in a dynamic partnership, the better your enjoyment and the better the quality of your tango. The more each one accepts the responsibility and consequence of each one's contribution to the dance, the faster you will dance freely and with a sense of yourself expressed. It is magic.

The fundamentals you learn and know and own now will serve you every day as a tango dancer. You will always use them. More intricate figures are only the fundamentals pushed to the maximum. Just as musicians and singers need to do scales, and ballet dancers need the same barre work they learned at age six until they retire, tango dancers use all the good and hard fundamental work they do in the first months for all their lives as tango dancers.

MASTERING FLOOR CRAFT

Floor craft is learning to exist in a prescribed space with other dancers, whether there are only 2 couples on the floor or 500 couples. You now know that the dance moves in a counterclockwise manner. You know that there is no literal line of dance; couples do not follow each other in a regimen of one after the other. Tango is not a conga line. You are not on a train. The dance is circular. The man dances around the floor, and the woman dances around the man. There are large circles and smaller ones. The dance floor resembles rings of an onion: There are multiple tracks. If the dancers apply the theories of moving in diagonals and dancing a few movements to the left and a few to the right, always alternating, they will have fewer problems.

Common sense rules, too. Compare your dancing to good driving. For instance, you can see the couple in front of you. If you see that couple stop or slow down, do you accelerate and crash your car into them? Floor craft, common sense, and good manners dictate that you tailor your movements to the couple dancing in front of you.

A commonly held belief is that good dancers prefer to dance on the periphery of the floor. Like most belief systems, this one defies the rule. Many dancers move to the inside to execute a fancy figure and then move out again into the flow. Many dancers get caught in the inner circulation and dance well there. The point is to dance well where you are and dance well enough to go where you want to go, inside or outside of the floor (or anything in between).

Full responsibility for circulation rests with the man, because he is generally moving forward, controlling the dance and marking the woman's movement. Of course, the woman must do her part to have control of herself (balance, axis, and connection). She must be sensible and not do inappropriate embellishments on a crowded floor or back herself into a collision. Still the general consensus is that the man needs to have the skill to mark everything and smoothly guide and control the woman's movements.

A traditional embrace compared to a modern embrace.

Embellishments

Sooner than later you will be visually attracted to the way some seasoned dancers seem to add another layer of expressiveness to their dancing. They use the whole body to interpret each piece of music, no matter which arrangement of a melody is played. What is it that they do that seems to enhance their dance?

In this book we have deliberately left out instructions on performing embellishments. However, you should know a few facts about them.

What is meant by the word *embellishment*? In the vernacular of the Argentine tango it is the action of adding a little something extra to the core movement of the body that produces the locomotion of the legs and feet.

Both women and men do embellishments. The addition to the core movement, the embellishing of a movement or step, is meant to be seamless. In terms of musical counts, it is movement within the main beat; it happens simultaneously within a step. As seen from the outside by someone with an uneducated eye, embellishments tend to look like the sole expression of a dancer's legs and feet. This is an oversimplification.

Embellishments should not be "learned," memorized, or copied. The mere replication of movements copied from an admired dancer, without a real understanding of what they mean, what they are used for, where they come from, and how they are crafted and created, will only produce insignificant and unpleasant results. Embellishments are not a just a woman's thing to be done without context. When the man knows how to guide and the woman knows how to be guided, and they both have a good ear for the music, each one of them may add embellishments with musical accuracy. There will be no disturbance to one another or any type of pull or vibration. Embellishments do not interfere with la marca (marking) of movements, steps, or sequences.

Unless the couple is dancing a prearranged choreography, the woman does not need to wait for the man to "give" her time if she wishes to embellish. While improvising, the woman relies on her intelligence, her ability, and her experience to know and decide if her movement corresponds to creating an embellishment. Dancers who have limited experience should be discouraged from attempting to embellish at a milonga; classes and practices are more appropriate places for acquiring technique and confidence.

Often, embellishments need and can be worked out technically and methodically. However, when it comes time to put them into action, they must be done spontaneously and appropriately. Both the individual and the couple will reflect their love and passion for the music of the Argentine tango when embellishments are created and used within the spirit of the dance.

The idea is to carry the personal space created by the two of you as if it were all the space you have. Consider that the dance was formed in very tight conditions in Buenos Aires. You might reason that if the dance floor on which you are dancing has more space, why not spread out and do big movements?

We like to think that the goal is to dance an authentic Argentine tango for the very reason that we are attracted to its unique posture and look. Lack of space dictated the formation of the shape and size of the embrace. Even if there is only one couple on the floor, Argentine tango is danced as if there were no extra space around a couple.

So logic will tell you that if you are going to use figures involving boleos or ganchos, you must keep them within the space you have. This means no big kicks or movements that can affect another couple. You can do boleos and ganchos if you understand alignment and keep in mind that the man keeps the woman hidden within the embrace. This goes back to the formative years of the tango, when a man hid the woman from the eyes of other men and protected her from any other bodies touching her, whether on purpose or by accident.

For every tradition there is a contradiction; for every effort to preserve the intrinsic values of the dance and foster its values, there is a teacher or a dancer pleading young and pushing the envelope to promote changes in posture, embrace, and the look that is so unique to the tango. It is not unusual to run into couples who dance so separated that they occupy the space normally occupied by four couples. Some movements are exaggerated cone shapes with the partners breaking the embrace in order to fall away from each other. These movements and postures occupy much more space than movements and postures from the past. As new things come up, they make their way onto the dance floor. If you are attracted to these designer moves, by all means do them with a skill that will not disturb the space of other dancers. However, nothing can take the place of the tango truly embraced—dancing close is dancing Argentine tango.

The Argentine tango is known as a dancer's dance. It affords the utmost experience for the couple dancing socially. The ability of one person to indicate motion to another and improvise movement for navigation requires thought and control of the body. The ability of the other person to be connected to herself and to her partner with finesse and to understand the concepts of axis, motion, lack of motion, and response in the moment is tremendous. While its core concepts are not difficult to understand, it is the one dance that cannot be faked or choreographed for the social dance floor. You must trust that you will be comfortable with yourself and with your partner. Reading about it, talking about it, watching a DVD, or going to class alone will not make you a tango dancer. Dancing tango makes you a tango dancer. The more you dance, the better it gets. So please go out and dance, and go out and dance often. The world of Argentine tango grows every day, yet at the same time the tango world becomes smaller because of travel, the Internet, and all media. It is a wonderful expression of human ability to embrace in the context of sociability and popular art forms of music and dance. We hope to meet you and dance with you and share our mutual healthy addiction.

CHAPTER 10

Beyond the Social Milieu

Then come the lights shining on you from above. You are a
performer. You forget all you learned, the process of technique, the
fear, the pain. You even forget who you are. You become one with
the music, the lights, indeed one with the dance.

—Shirley MacLaine

Dancing Argentine tango socially is an equal-opportunity endeavor.
Everyone at any age is capable of doing it. It is an urban dance to
music that was created primarily for the pleasure of dancers in all
levels of the porteño society halfway through the 19th century. With the passing
of the years, new generations of musicians educated in conservatories wrote
music, and writers who came from universities became the poets of the tango
lyric. Likewise, in our current era of the tango dance, many dancers who have
trained classically, or in folklore dance academies in Argentina, have taken up
Argentine tango as a profession. At no other time in the history of the dance
have there been more teachers and professional performers.

SHOW DANCING

Dancing for the stage is different from dancing socially. The first obvious difference is that there is a set and rehearsed choreography. Depending on the
level of dancer, show dancing is something that nonprofessional dancers can
also get into. You can seek out classes that are given for that specific purpose.
If your teacher doesn't currently offer classes in show tango, ask for it. You
can take the movements and figures you know from the social floor and adapt
them to your own choreography. Make sure you understand the difference
between show tango and social tango. At the social level, dancers dance for
each other, sharing the intimacy of their own space and time. Exhibitions,
performances, and showcases are meant for an audience that agrees to sit
down and watch you.

Since there are not enough performance opportunities for the wealth of
professional couples we are now seeing, if you want to perform your show
tango at the amateur level, you may have to create your own showcase. Many

communities welcome free shows at nursing homes and school assemblies. Some ballroom schools, clubs, and organizations might let you do an exhibition if it does not conflict with their interests. Clubs you belong to may be curious to see what you are doing with your free time, and they might invite you to dance a tango or two for an event or social get-together. Myriad benefits for charities often need a free floor show. Your tango teacher may want to present a group of students to encourage more people to come to classes and build the tango dance community.

You can also ask the organizers of your milongas if they might make time in the evening for one or two couples to dance for the group (you can even use your improvisational dance skills for this type of exhibition). You can always find an audience that will be curious to see what the tango is all about. You'll make your own showcase opportunities.

If you are in peak physical condition, you may seek training to become a bona fide professional stage dancer. Some tango shows tour sporadically on the international level. There are a few nightclub-style shows in Buenos Aires. Tango festivals often hire professional show dancers. Realistically, there are few opportunities for the talent pool of professional stage dancers in Argentine tango. However, if your goal is to become a professional show dancer, be prepared to spend many hours in training. Most professional dancers rehearse for at least four hours per day. They cross-train with daily ballet or

Show dancing as performed on stage.

jazz classes. They go to the gym and take yoga or Pilates for physical strength training. It is a full-time job.

If dancing professionally is your dream, then by all means do it. Again, you will need to seek coaching and training from a professional. You might start with your local instructors and go as far as you can with them. Established show dancers may want to supplement their income with private coaching. You may want to spend a few months in Buenos Aires (a wonderful place to develop your social dance skills) and seek out coaching for show tango.

TANGO COMPETITION

The question of competition at both the amateur and professional levels has been raised. In the ballroom world, competition is a well-established part of the system. Argentine tango has been perceived as a romantic and idealistic dance of emotional expression or as something free and so highly individual that it can't possibly be judged in a competition. While it is true that the tango involves you at an emotional level, the art of improvisation guides its movements, and each one dancing has a unique look, those factors should not exclude the possibility of competition.

Some competitions have been held in the United States. Some local USABDA (United States of America Ballroom Dance Association) chapters have included Argentine tango. A competition including professionals and amateurs was held in Miami in conjunction with a privately organized tango congress. Years ago in Los Angeles a competition was held that was connected with an event to honor Carlos Gardel at Paramount Studios. It was a publicity vehicle that attracted only six couples in a city of millions. Because this idea of Argentine tango competition is in its infancy, and it is still met with resistance or a lack of interest from the majority of social dancers, it is hardly a blip on the radar screen. People come away with trophies and medals that are meaningless because they might be the only couple entered in a category. Glitzy professionals are assured of a win to give a name to an organizer's event. Some competitions are announced with great fanfare, press releases, Internet teasers, and fancy posters, only to fizzle when no one shows up to compete. There was even a fellow who came up with the idea of producing a syllabus so that Argentine tango could be considered for Olympic competition as dance sport. This proposal met with little enthusiasm from dancers and no reaction from the International Olympic Committee. Until social dancers feel the value of putting what they know on the public line, organized competition will not fly.

Competitions in Argentina attract serious, trained, and talented dancers from Argentina as well as from around the world. Seasoned social dancers from Argentina also compete in their categories. International couples are going there to compete alongside Argentine dancers. For the most part, these are privately organized tie-ins to tango festivals, although the government of the city of Buenos Aires has taken a major interest in sponsoring world championships of tango because of the significant tourist revenue involved. With each passing year the competitions in and around Buenos Aires are gaining respect and credibility. Although it is an accomplishment to step onto the floor anywhere, the knowing eyes of the Argentine culture behind the judging of competitions there is uniquely valuable. For many who compete anywhere in the world, the value of the prize is very personal. Champions in the show and professional categories in Argentina gather credible accolades and valuable jobs in shows or festivals worldwide.

The question also arises about who will judge a competition and by what standard. Teachers who come from training in ballroom dance have made isolated attempts to write a syllabus for Argentine tango without understanding that it is a unique dance outside their current system. Again, the cries from the purists took the form of "How can you judge my style and a feeling?" As in beauty contests, some judges are celebrities adding their names for a fee. In Argentina, generally the competition judges are respected and recognized dance professionals.

International tango competition in Buenos Aires.

Official Rules of Tango Dance World Championships in Argentina

Salon Tango (Unrestricted Entry, Amateurs and Professionals)

1. Once a couple is formed, the partners shall not separate as long as the music is playing. This means that they cannot break the embrace, which is considered the tango dance position.

2. For the position to be considered correct, the partners must constantly hold each other by means of the embrace. During certain figures this may be flexible, but deviating from the embrace should not continue throughout the entire piece.

3. All movements shall be performed within the space allowed by the couple's embrace.

4. The jury will give special relevance to the couple's musicality, elegance, and walking style.

5. Within these guidelines, participants may perform any figure commonly used, including barridas, sacadas close to the floor, and enrosques.

6. Ganchos, leaps, trepadas (climbs), and any other typical stage-tango moves are completely excluded.

7. Couples, as in a real dance hall, shall constantly move counterclockwise and avoid remaining in the same place for more than two musical measures.

8. No contestant may raise his or her legs above the knee line.

Stage Tango for Couples (Unrestricted Entry, Amateurs and Professionals)

1. Participants will be able to express their personal view on the tango dance: They may resort to movements, figures, and applications that are not usually related to traditional tango.

2. Couples may break the embrace and use additional techniques derived from other dance disciplines as long as these are done in the context of the tango and performed for the benefit of a particular rendition.

3. In reference to the previous clause, no performances using a different dance technique to dance to tango music shall be accepted.

The jury will take into account the following criteria:

- Choreographic composition (creation or re-creation)
- Preservation of tango essence
- Use of stage space
- Choreographic and postural techniques
- Body and spatial alignment
- Couple's synchronicity
- Choreographic effects
- Interpretation
- Musical accuracy (relaxation, the relationship of the music to the dancers, and the style of the tango being shown—tango, vals, or milonga)
- Costumes and makeup

Translated from www.mundialdetango.gov.ar/reglamento.php.

BECOMING A TEACHER

In the world of Argentine tango, sometimes it seems that there are more social dance teachers than students and dancers. The odds for a new woman showing up at a tango dance party and being given express tango lessons right on the floor are very high. The attraction that some people have to teaching cannot be denied. How does one become a teacher of Argentine tango?

There are no college or university courses. There are no officially sanctioned programs. There is no official or sanctioned certification. Several enterprises exist claiming exclusive training methods and delivering official-looking certifications for a fee. At times the process of becoming a teacher seems like a free-for-all with no standards. Yet, we know when a good teacher leaves a lasting impression in our lives. For now, common sense and integrity must rule.

If you are a good communicator, if you have a comprehensive understanding of the structure of the dance, if you have a complete knowledge of the music, if you have knowledge and respect for the Argentine culture and knowledge of the history and environment that formed the dance, if you have solid skills as a dancer, and if you have the time to dedicate to teaching, then perhaps teaching is for you. Acquiring all these skills is a process that you will have to undertake on your own. Business skills come into play too. Classes need to have a dollar value put on them. Studio space must be found and paid for. Advertising for classes needs to happen. Don't underestimate or overlook the value this book has for the aspiring teacher as well.

STANDARDS OF EXCELLENCE FOR ARGENTINE TANGO

Of course there is a high standard for dancing Argentine tango. While it is a dance of the people and for the people, it has a level of difficulty that must be reckoned with. There is a structure of the dance from whence improvisation is created. There is a learning curve and a developmental curve that comes from putting in hours that lead to weeks that lead to years of taking classes and dancing socially. Even the uninitiated eye of a newcomer can look at a room full of tango dancers and see various levels of ability. Most important is that those who dance Argentine tango hold themselves to their own standards of excellence. The judgment of self is the most rigorous!

This go-around of the Argentine tango is still new. For the first time in the history of the tango, more people outside of Argentina than inside of Argentina are dancing the tango. Those who are not natives of Argentina are evolving and taking small steps that deal with a culture that is not their own, trying to make it a meaningful experience. Regardless of nationality, the tango lifestyle requires great effort and commitment. It is difficult to learn to dance, to learn the music, and to socialize. Be aware of opportunists who, while outwardly banging the drum for the Argentine dancers, devise ways to remove most things Argentine, the essence that once nourished them.

Inside Argentina the evolution is taking place as older dancers pass on and the younger dancers try to revamp the dance to make it their own. The poignant hug of an older milonguero can be appreciated as much as the forceful dance of the younger dancer. All these tender feelings will sort themselves out, and perhaps there will come a day when dancers of Argentine tango will have a mature confidence that might allow the dance to become an Olympic sport or maybe just a friendly contest in a neighborhood milonga that nets the winner a bottle of champagne and bragging rights.

With evolution will come preservation of the Argentine tango (music, culture, poetry, and dance) that has been formed over the last hundred years. Today there are living witnesses of a tango covenant that has bonded generations of men and women in the mission of preserving what we love; seeing to its preservation when we are gone; and exposing all attempts to distort it, exploit it, and destroy it.

The ones who started this current cycle of the tango in the 1980s had a heartfelt mission to foster and preserve the Argentine tango. Now, halfway through the first decade of the 21st century, some are becoming dinosaurs or simply dying out. We will not live long enough to see the rose planted firmly again in alternative teeth. The tango seems to need to die only to be reborn. We and many of our friends, associates, and disciples work hard to make sure that when someone wants to see the relics of the Argentine tango, our archives will be intact, and someone much like us will once again see the beauty and excitement of it and make it live. It could be you. . .

Glossary

abrazo—Embrace. The tango hug.

aguja—Needle. An adornment for the man. It is done with the free foot vertical and the toe into the floor while pivoting on the support leg.

amague—From *amagar*. A deceptive motion such as stepping in one direction and immediately going in the opposite direction. The man uses it to mark a lady's boleo.

apilado—Piled on. A form of embracing that resembles the way a jockey is "piled" on top of his horse when racing—hugging the neck.

arrastre—From *arrastrar*, to drag.

arrepentida—A change of mind. Evasive actions that allow a couple to back away from a collision or traffic jam in a minimal amount of space and on short notice.

¿bailamos?—Informal for "Shall we dance?"

bailar—To dance.

bailarin—A dedicated dancer.

bailemos— "Let's dance."

bailongo—A tango slang word to describe a place where people dance (a milonga).

bandoneón—A concertina looking reed musical instrument originally created as a portable pipe organ for music for outdoor religious activities in Germany. It has the appearance of a box with bellows with two sets of buttons, one for each hand. It first appeared in Buenos Aires toward the last decade of the 19th century and gradually began to replace the flute and clarinet in tango trios, becoming the lead instrument of choice for expressing the sound of the Argentine tango.

barrida—A sweep. A sweeping motion in which the dancers' feet travel together during the opening that follows a back step of the person whose foot is being "swept." It is an illusion, and feet don't actually push each other. They follow the action of the upper bodies.

base—A figure that consists of the three unique steps each leg can execute: a lateral (opening), a forward, and a back with either leg. When done in the dancing position, it renders a parallelogram pattern similar to the baldosa.

boleo—The action of interrupting an outside cross, converting it to an inside cross, or vice versa.

cabeceo—A nod of the head signifying "Shall we dance?" prevalent at the traditional dance halls of Buenos Aires. The gesture is used by the man to invite a lady to dance from a distance when the lady allows eye contact to be made. A lady's nodding of the head, or any other barely perceptible facial movement, indicates "Yes, you may dance with me."

cadena—Chain. A series of sequences linked to each other and repeated several times.

cadencia—A swaying motion of the body following the cadence of the music.

calesita—Carousel. A figure in which the man walks around the woman, keeping her centered over, and pivoting on, axis.

cambio—Change. Cambio de frente, or change of front; cambio de dirección, or change of direction; and cambio de parejas, change of partners.

caminada—A sequence of three or four steps that results in the displacement of the couple along the line of dance.

caminar—To walk.

canyengue—A certain attitude displayed by young men indicating lack of interest for formalities and authorities circa 1900. A way to dance the tango mimicking the gait and posture of the canyengue demeanor of some youth. A rhythmic effect created by hitting the strings of the upright bass with the hand or the arch of the bow.

carpa—Tent. A figure created when the man keeps the lady on one foot and then steps back away from her, causing her body to rest at a soft V-shaped angle on the right side of his body. Sometimes affectionately known as *adormecida*, as the man "puts her to sleep, calming her down," before continuing to dance.

chiche—Toy. An embellishment done in place with the feet close together in time with the beat.

club style—A way to dance in the crowded clubs in the center of Buenos Aires.

codigo—Code of The Tango. A repetitive and predictable way for the woman to dance around the man.

codigos—Codes. The set of demanding codes of conduct and courtesy that prevail in the milongas in Buenos Aires.

colgada—From *colgar*, to hang. A turn on a shared axis resulting in an inverted cone shape as the dancers hang away from each other.

compás—Beat. The main pulse that defines the tempo of the music.

contrapaso—Skip. Stepping twice with the same foot by changing weight when the feet come together.

corrida—From *correr*, to run. Also *corridita*, little run. A short sequence, usually done in groups of three quick steps.

corte—Cut. An interruption of movement, such as at the end of a salida, or the third step of the resolution when both feet come together for a change of weight in place.

cortina—Curtain. A brief musical interlude of a totally different genre between tandas.

cross-feet system—The couple steps together using the same foot instead of the opposite as in parallel system.

cruzada—From *cruzar*, to cross. The action of crossing the legs.

cunita—Cradle. A sequence of forward and backward rocking steps.

eight-count giro—A turning sequence consisting of eight body positions and displacements.

enrosque—From *enroscar*, to coil or twist the legs.

espejo—Mirror. Mirroring the body position of one's partner.

firulete—Adornment; decoration; embellishment. A drawing or writing on the floor with the free foot.

freno—Stop and hold; brake.

gancho—Leg hook.

giro—Turn.

la marca—The indication used by the man of when, where, and how the woman moves into the space he creates.

lapiz—Pencil. An embellishment that looks like a number 6 drawn on the floor using the free foot as if it was a pencil.

lento—Slow.

llevada—From *llevar*, to carry. A displacement provoked by moving into the woman's free leg that carries her leg to the next step.

media luna—Half moon. One of the oldest figures in the tango.

media vuelta—Half turn.

milonga—May refer to the music, written in 6/8 time, or to the dance itself, or to the dance salon where people go to dance tango, or to a tango dance party.

milonguero (masculine; feminine milonguera)—Refers to those frequenting the milongas and whose lifestyle revolves around dancing tango and the philosophy of tango.

milonguita—A diminutive word for a short tango dance party. Also a name given to a young woman who worked the cabarets in search of a rich man to take care of her.

molinete—Windmill. An old turning figure in which the lady dances around the man who serves as an anchor or center axis for her rotation.

mordida—To bite. The woman's action of clearing the man's foot if he places it on the outside of her foot instead of the inside, in giro 6 to the left or to the right.

noche—Night.

ocho—Eight. Figure eight. The ocho, forward or back, is a direction change to the man's left and right (or vice versa), provoked while the woman takes either a forward or a back step.

orquesta—Orchestra. An 11-piece tango ensemble.

palanca—Lever; leverage. Describes the subtle assisting of the woman by the man during jumps or lifts in tango fantasia (stage tango).

parada—Stop. The man stops the woman, usually as she crosses back.

parallel system—When the dancers step with opposite feet. His left, her right, and so on.

pareja—Couple. The two partners in a tango.

pasada—Passing over.

paso—Step.

patada—Kick.

pausa—Pause; wait. Holding a position or pose for two or more beats of music.

pecho—Chest.

pie—Foot.

pierna—Leg.

pinta—Appearance; presentation. Includes clothes, grooming, posture, expression, and manner of speaking and relating to the world.

piso—Floor.

pista—Dance floor.

planeo—Glide.

porteño (feminine porteña)—An inhabitant of the port city of Buenos Aires.

postura—Posture.

práctica—An informal practice session for tango dancers.

quebrada—Break; broken. A posture in which the body breaks at the waist and uses a deep bend of the knees.

rabona—A lock step produced by crossing a foot behind the other with the intent of kicking.

resolución—Resolution; tango close.

ritmo—Rhythm.

rodillas—Knees.

ronda—The imaginary line of dance. Etiquette requires the dance couple to move around in a counterclockwise direction using diagonals in concentric lanes to facilitate navigation in proximity with other couples.

rulo—A curl drawn on the floor with the free foot.

sacada— From *sacar*. Displacement.

salida—From *salir*, to exit; to go out. Derived from "¿Salimos a bailar?" [Shall we (go out to the dance floor) and dance?]. Also a four-step figure done on a diagonal to the man's left side ending at the woman's cruzada position.

seguidillas—Tiny quick steps used in a corrida.

sentada—From *sentar*, to sit. A sitting action. A family of figures in which the woman creates the illusion of sitting on, or actually mounting, the man's leg.

suave—Smooth, steady, and gentle. Soft, stylish, and dense.

syncopation—The action of doing the unexpected, such as stepping when it is not expected or not stepping when it is expected.

tanda—A set of dance music, usually three or four songs of the same dance in similar style and often by the same orchestra or another orchestra in the same mode.

tanguero (feminine tanguera)—Refers to anyone who has a significant interest in any or all aspects of the tango, including the dance, the music, the poetry, the history, and the plastic arts.

trabada—Lock. A locked step as in the cruzada or the rabona.

traspie—Contrapaso. Stepping twice with the same foot. Usually used to change to and from the cross-feet system. As a matter of choice, the traspie can be executed on a slow or quick step.

vaiven—As in *va* (go) *y* (and) *ven* (come). A change of front using a rock step.

vals—Argentine waltz. The music is referred to as *vals criollo*, and the dance as *vals cruzado*.

volcada—From *volcar*, to lean forward. The action of tilting the lady's axis.

zarandeo—Swing. A quick sequence of hip pivots with both thighs together, resulting in small swivels of the feet in place.

About the Authors

Alberto Paz and **Valorie Hart** own Planet Tango, a company dedicated to preserving, fostering, and advancing the traditional values of Argentine tango culture, with a school and tango salon located in New Orleans, Louisiana. They produce the widely successful New Orleans TangoFest each year. Together, Paz and Hart conduct master Argentine tango classes as well as lectures and workshops in cities across America and the world. They also publish *El Firulete*, an online international Argentine tango magazine in English, and they have been featured dancers on the Buenos Aires TV show *Tango Around the World*. With

their Web site, www.planet-tango.com, Paz and Hart provide dancers the opportunity to network on an international level.

Paz is a native of Argentina and grew up in the city of Buenos Aires, while Hart was born in the United States and is ballet trained with experience in both off-Broadway and summer stock. The two met in 1995 during a tango conference and workshop at Stanford University. Since then, the pair has made Argentine tango dancing their business.

They have developed a methodology based on the fundamental structure of the dance, combining traditional and modern concepts of improvisation originally developed in the 1930s, updated in the 1990s, and successfully utilized in workshops in cities across America and around the world since 1997.